RICE'S LANGUAGE of BUILDINGS

RICE'S
LANGUAGE
OF BUILDINGS

BLOOMSBURY PUBLISHING
LONDON · OXFORD · NEW YORK · NEW DELHI · SYDNEY

First published in Great Britain in 2009 as *Rice's Architectural Primer*
This edition published in Great Britain in 2018

Text and illustrations copyright © 2009 and 2018 by Matthew Rice

Expanded from a series of architectural cribs commissioned
by and published in *Country Life*.

Bloomsbury Publishing Plc, 50 Bedford Square, London WC1B 3DP
29 Earlsfort Terrace, Dublin 2, Ireland

Bloomsbury Publishing, London, Oxford, New Delhi, New York and Sydney

A CIP catalogue record for this book is available from the British Library.

ISBN 978 1 4088 9378 4

10 9 8 7 6 5 4 3

Design: Grade Design Consultants www.gradedesign.com

Printed and bound in China by C&C Offset Printing Co., Ltd.

All papers used by Bloomsbury Publishing are natural, recyclable products
made from wood grown in well-managed forests. The manufacturing processes
conform to the environmental regulations of the country of origin.

www.bloomsbury.com

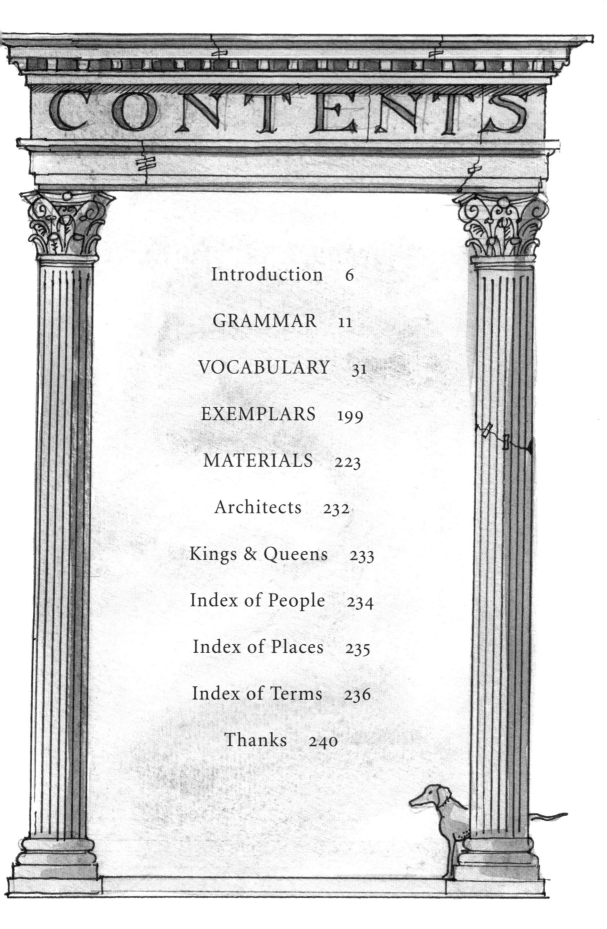

CONTENTS

INTRODUCTION

This is the second introduction I have written to this book. The first one seemed just right when I started, but having finished the work, I saw I hadn't understood the half of it. Because, wherever you look, wherever you go and whatever you are doing, with the possible exception of ocean sailing, ARCHITECTURE is all around. It is the backdrop to our lives. The brilliant, awful, thrilling or dreary walls that enclose us, the doors we walk through, the church we are married in or see our grandparents buried in, the shops we walk past on the way to the station that we board the train at, all are architecture.

I had used a rather trite line about being able to leave a cathedral with as much to talk about as after seeing a feature film and that this book would give you the vocabulary to do so. But it was a poor comparison because you never need to go to the cinema (more architecture), but you will always, ALWAYS see buildings. Not being able to describe the middle of Oxford, the walk from the Tate Modern to Blackfriars underground station or Durham Cathedral is like not knowing the wheels of your car from the bonnet. It is that central to our lives.

With that rather breathless beginning out of the way, it is worth remarking that, although cars have been about for only one hundred years, there has been sophisticated architecture in Britain for fourteen hundred years – in fact even longer – if you count the buildings of the Romans. From the Saxons and the much more visible NORMANS, through the GOTHIC, the RENAISSANCE, the BAROQUE and PALLADIANISM to the frantic revisiting of all these styles in the reign of QUEEN VICTORIA, and the cool austerity of MODERNISM, there is simply so much material.

This book is not a history of architecture. Each chapter begins with an introduction to the period, but only to put in context the drawings that follow. These are of buildings, or parts of buildings, mainly unnamed, and are purely to illustrate the LANGUAGE of the age. DRAWINGS are better than photographs for this because so much can be left out. You can thus concentrate on one or two key features. So if you recognise your house or church and a window or door is missing, please do not panic or feel offended. PLANS are as important as ELEVATIONS and have been included, as have some elements of construction where they remain visible, but this remains principally a book of DETAILS and external decoration and features.

Architecture is a reflection of the political events of its age, foreign policy, war, strife and conquest. It is a reaction to travel, literature and theological passions, and is the physical manifestation of changing schools of thought. It is a weapon of imperialism and a symbol of power. In the nineteenth century, the style was chosen to fit the purpose of the building: the echoes of ancient Rome, classical Greece or the Christian might of the Gothic invested the stones of which they were built with the values of the societies from which they derived. The neo-Classical porch of a suburban bungalow, even if it is made of uPVC, is imbuing that villa with the might of Imperial Rome. It is no coincidence that it is a form of decoration favoured in the sprawling suburbs of the United States. Similarly, a new and feature-less red-brick box of a church will sport a Gothic arch somewhere as SHORTHAND for 'This IS a church, whatever you may think'.

Single books, by Vitruvius, Serlio or Ruskin, have changed the face of our architecture. Lord Caernarvon and Howard Carter's discovery of the TOMB OF TUTANKHAMUN in 1922 was reflected in the façades of scores of factories and cinemas, and the horror of the GREAT WAR was the death knell of the revival styles of the nineteenth century.

The early part of the book is heavy on the ECCLESIASTICAL. This reflects the importance and status of the Church in medieval Britain, until the advent of the TUDORS marked a change, occasionally a sudden one, towards the SECULAR, and the grandee's house in particular. The rise of democracy brings with it a move towards CIVIC buildings, and the eventual triumph of unbridled capitalism is reflected in a move towards commercial projects as the focus of great architecture. Few contemporary buildings are such advanced feats of architectural engineering as the Selfridges store in Birmingham.

This is not a book concerned with REGIONALISM. Most regional differences are reflections of the change in the architectural vernacular; that is, the way in which a building reflects the local materials, weather, economic conditions and customs of building. This is construction not by architects, but by builders and house owners for whom the style of the elevations is not the principal concern. However, in the chapter of EXEMPLARS, the houses chosen should allow all readers to explore the changes in architectural styles close at hand.

I have tried to include at least one sample of every period in each part of Great Britain and, where possible, to use those examples that are easily visible from the public road or open to the public. Of course, the CITIES have more buildings of architectural significance than other parts of the country (except Birmingham or others scarred by bombing and the pernicious town planning of the immediate post-war years). As LONDON grew exponentially faster than its competitors, it also gained architectural precedence. It was not until the second phase of the Industrial Revolution in the mid-nineteenth century that the northern metropolis of Manchester began to challenge the capital, or that other regional centres – Liverpool, Bradford and Leeds or Glasgow – began to grow to their current size. For hundreds of years, Norwich and then Bristol was Britain's second city. Some cities, such as Bath, have outstanding buildings from one or two periods, but not others.

It is easy to forget that architectural touring can be SEASONAL. For obvious reasons of muddy feet and chilly conditions, the National Trust and many other organisations do not open from late October until Easter. Although this is often very annoying, it is understandable, so it is always worth checking first to avoid disappointment. It is also worth bearing in mind that it is often the outside only that one wants to see, and that this is accessible for more of the year. Similarly, some CHURCHES that are kept open all day in the summer clang shut their doors for the winter. It is usually easy to find the key-holder (there may be a note pinned in the porch indicating where the key is), but do remember that many churches with marvellous exteriors are grim within. Excessive restoration over the past 150 years can make the interior a disappointment. Clamber up and peer through the church window for a look before rousing a sleeping granny from her fireside to let you in. If you do visit churches, don't forget to leave a donation. Nearly all churches are desperately short of money, and a pound or two from every visitor makes a real difference.

Draw and take photographs to help you remember what you have seen. Drawing is best, however ham-fisted, because the time spent recording helps to fix the image in your mind. Failing this, your own photographs are always more useful than somebody else's. It is strange, but true, that people very rarely photograph a building face on.

Architecture is FIRST among the APPLIED ARTS, filtering down to furniture and on to ceramics or silverware. Its fashions are reflected in book illustration and industrial design; indeed, many architects also work in these subsidiary fields. LEARN the LANGUAGE so you can communicate. Not, of course, with the buildings or with the architects themselves, but with your friends or children.

This is a book to help you avoid having to stumble through a description of *that bit with knobbles and a point,* or *the curved thing to the left of that triangle* by teaching you the NAMING OF PARTS, which will give you a real familiarity with any building you may be in.

These first pages are about the Grammar of Architecture and some of the BASIC COMPONENTS. These are the things that crop up again and again through the ages, elements that are reused as styles, are developed and revived, and that are borrowed and adopted by architects of every period. Certain features of both principal architectural styles, the CLASSICAL (the way of building that derives from that used in ancient Rome) and the GOTHIC (the pointed style that began in Europe in the twelfth century), recur in this way. The Classical, much simplified and pared down in the economically backward Dark Ages, gave us the columns and capitals and barrel vaults of the ROMANESQUE or NORMAN, and then reappeared via the Italian Renaissance, reaching us in the sixteenth century. From then on, the COLUMN, the PEDIMENT, the CORNICE and the ROUNDED ARCH have never completely left the stage. The Gothic style, which reached its first peak in the great cathedrals of medieval Britain, continued in one or another diluted form from the sixteenth century to the early nineteenth century, until Augustus Pugin and his successors raised it again to a period of prominence in Victoria's reign. But all this time, the LANCET and the OGEE, the TREFOIL and the QUATRE-FOIL, CRESTING and CROCKETING continued to form visually significant parts of British buildings, even if they were derided and scorned by a large part of the architectural establishment.

Perhaps GRAMMAR is a bad word. It implies a strict set of rules that must be obeyed, a series of systems and proportions from which the slightest deviation should be avoided. Architectural theorists have imposed many such strictures. The great ORDERS of architecture – DORIC, TUSCAN, IONIC, CORINTHIAN and COMPOSITE – are one such set of prescriptions, but, in reality, each recitation of the orders – Serlio, Michelangelo, Palladio or Chambers – varies significantly. Indeed, individual architects play and invent using these toys. Sir John Vanbrugh broke every rule in his great palaces in the seventeenth century, and Charles Cockerell's use of the Ionic at the Ashmolean Museum in Oxford would have been anathema to William Kent or the fierce neo-Classicists who were his immediate predecessors.

BUT IF THERE ARE NO RULES… you cannot break them, and where's the fun in that? The innovations of the different schools of Classical architecture, the early Palladianism of Inigo Jones, Christopher Wren's Baroque or the austere Grecianism of William Wilkins, need to be seen as deviations from a norm to be fully understood. Here are some rules. The ROMANS had five ORDERS: Tuscan, Doric, Ionic, Corinthian, and Composite. The Doric, Ionic and Corinthian were also used by the ancient Greeks, although their versions are a little different. Each order includes a COLUMN with a CAPITAL and FOOT, and has a particular ENTABLATURE, which is the part of the building that the column supports. The entablature comprises a CORNICE, a FRIEZE and an ARCHITRAVE. These parts are further broken down into smaller components, as I have illustrated in the next few pages.

When you see such details as TORUS and SCOTIA you might wonder why each and every tiny part needs to have its name learnt, but the more you look at particular buildings and their peculiarities, the more you will see that it is the exaggerations, omissions or manipulations of these minor parts that give a building its particular character. If you can't name these details, you can't describe what is so odd or exciting about them.

Similarly, there are norms of PROPORTION. The length of a column's shaft varies according to its order. The length of a Doric or Tuscan column (the lowest of the orders) is seven times the width of the shaft at its base, the more refined and feminine Ionic column is eight times, and the most sophisticated Corinthian and the rather silly Composite columns are nine times.

More esoteric is INTERCOLUMNIATION. This is the distance between individual columns, which is also measured in multiples of the diameter of the columns at their base. Different intercolumniations have names too: PYCNOSTYLE means 1½ times; SYSTYLE 2 times; the most common EUSTYLE 2¼ times; DIASTYLE 3 times and AREOSTYLE 4 times or more. These may seem plain silly, but they have a huge impact on the elevation of a building and, indeed, a great effect on the actual experience of using that building.

Classical buildings are based on TEMPLES or TRIUMPHAL ARCHES, or other more particular buildings of the Ancients, such as baths or theatres. Often a building quotes directly from one of these, and this quotation is referred to in descriptions, such as: 'Using the Ionic order from the Temple of Boris in Southkenia.' These direct quotations were seen as an indemnification of a design and as proof of their correctness. From the temple comes the PEDIMENT, the triangular top, which can sometimes be curved (segmental) or have its apex missing (broken). From the triumphal arch comes the particular arrangement of columns and arches. These might be PILASTERS (thin slivers of columns fully adhered to the face of a building) or ENGAGED or PARTIALLY ENGAGED columns. To make their forms clear I have illustrated these in the groundplan on page 24. From the Colosseum, among other buildings, comes the system of precedence, one order over another, from Doric to Corinthian.

All these features will appear many times in this book in many forms, but they are all key items and worth memorising.

The GOTHIC part of architecture is rather different. There were, at least until the late-eighteenth and nineteenth centuries, no actual rule books. Gothic was a living style whose forms reflected its method of construction to a greater extent. VAULTING, first barrel, then groin, lierne and tierceron, each time gaining more and finer ribs, led at last to the filigree triumph of the fan vault. This progression matched the change through the styles subsequently named Romanesque or Norman, Early English, Decorated and Perpendicular, and the introduction of different shaped arches, first round, then pointed or lancet, then broader equilateral, and, finally, two or four shallower centred arches. It is worth remembering that these styles did not replace one another with convenient cut-off dates; indeed, they often co-existed, sometimes for up to a hundred years.

The earliest decoration was muscular and geometric: crosses, dog's tooth, bizarre and grotesque birds' beaks. The foliate natural forms of Romanesque capitals on squat Norman columns are still derived from the Corinthian order. That there is in fact an unbroken progression from Classical into Gothic via the Romanesque can be seen in the early churches in Rome, where actual ancient capitals were reused in seventh- and eighth-century basilicas. However, when seen in a cold and stark Norman parish church, the Roman Forum seems a long way away, and those leaves seem less a debased acanthus scroll than the curled oak leaves forming the hair of a green man, that slightly threatening pagan male face that snarls from carved-oak bosses in the roofs of church or cloister.

One of the most noticeable components of Gothic architecture is the TOWER or SPIRE. These are often a marriage of convenience between pragmatic needs of defence and a desire to be visible from a distance, reaching up to heaven. Several forms of spire, illustrated on pages 28–9, are attached to our churches. Some are plain spikes, some decorated with crocketing – gnarled, leaf-formed protrusions that mark the spire as it rises. Sometimes the line of the spire is broken or broached, or a smaller spire grows out of the top of a tower.

Pages 26–7 are concerned with some DECORATIVE elements. These are devices that are employed in buildings of all ages, but which, at certain times, were particularly well used. The Vitruvian scroll and the guilloche are both signal decorative elements typical of Palladian architecture, as is the Greek key. Other MOTIFS, such as cresting, were used as a shorthand for Gothic. In the eighteenth and early nineteenth centuries, buildings of perfectly Classical proportion and form were made 'Gothick' by the inclusion of these elements.

Page 16 shows a building divided into its component sections: STOREYS (horizontal divisions) and BAYS (vertical). These are important terms because they are an easy way to begin your description of a structure: 'Inigo Jones's Prince's Lodging at Newmarket was a seven-bay building of three storeys, bays three, four and five projecting under a pediment.' A storey above the cornice is called an attic storey. The lowest storey, above or below ground level, is the basement. The first floor, often with the windows heightened, is called the piano nobile.

These are the most BASIC terms for describing buildings of any type, and you will find that they will be really useful.

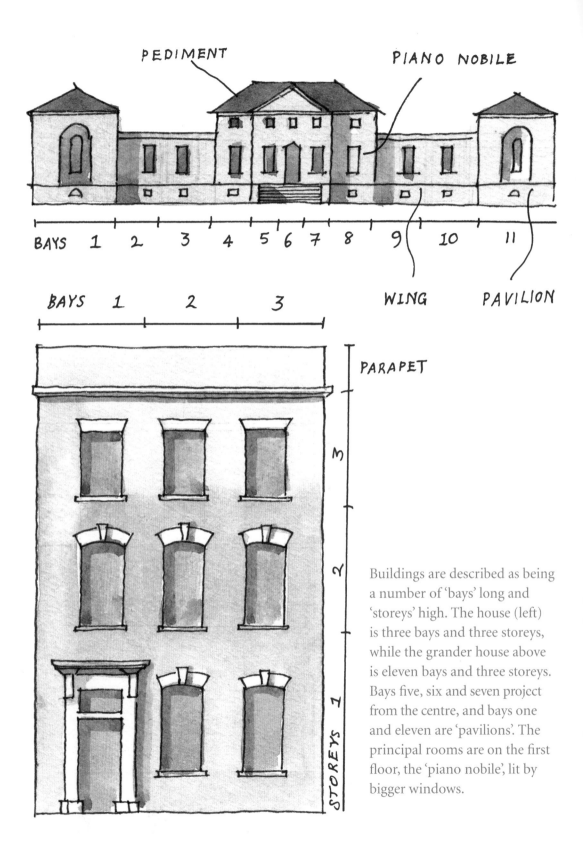

PEDIMENT

PIANO NOBILE

BAYS 1 2 3 4 5 6 7 8 9 10 11

BAYS 1 2 3

WING PAVILION

PARAPET

3

2

STOREYS 1

Buildings are described as being a number of 'bays' long and 'storeys' high. The house (left) is three bays and three storeys, while the grander house above is eleven bays and three storeys. Bays five, six and seven project from the centre, and bays one and eleven are 'pavilions'. The principal rooms are on the first floor, the 'piano nobile', lit by bigger windows.

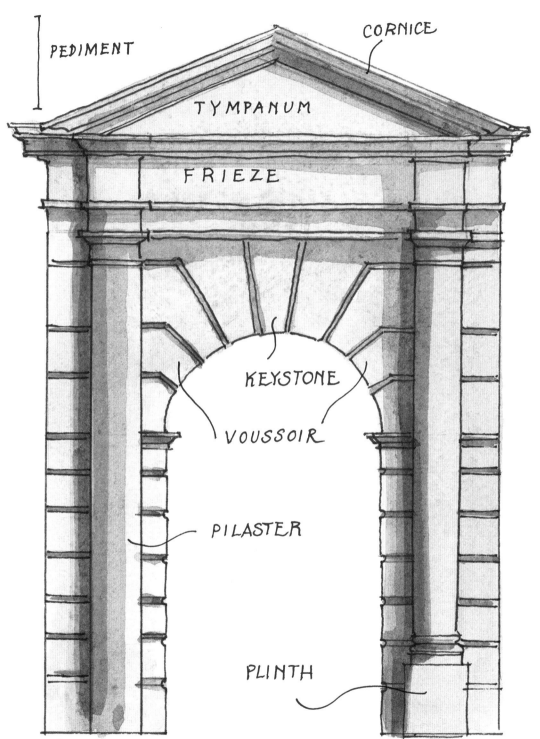

PEDIMENT

CORNICE

TYMPANUM

FRIEZE

KEYSTONE

VOUSSOIR

PILASTER

PLINTH

THIS WHOLE THING IS CALLED an AEDICULE

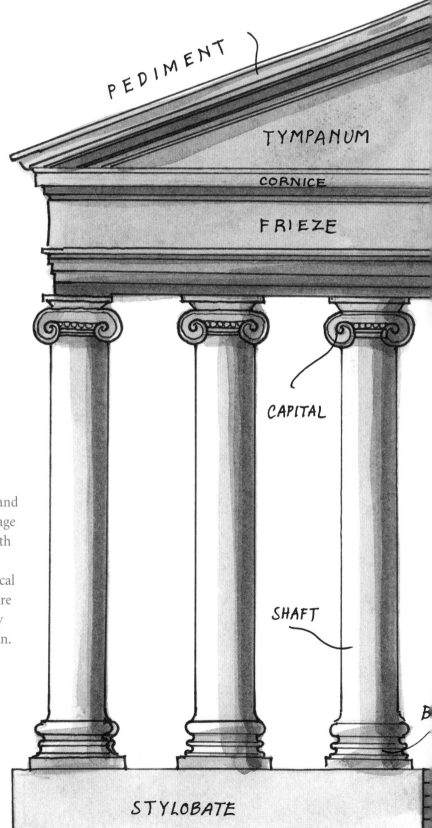

PEDIMENT

TYMPANUM

CORNICE

FRIEZE

CAPITAL

Here are two Classical types. The one on this page is a 'temple front' and the one on the facing page is a 'triumphal arch'. Both are Roman forms and reappear in most Classical buildings. These parts are the ones to learn as they come up again and again.

SHAFT

B

STYLOBATE

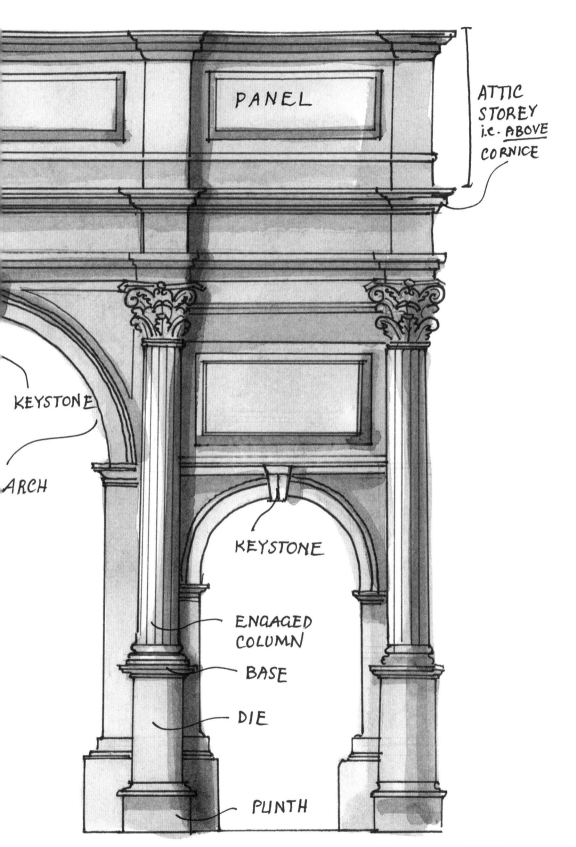

PANEL

ATTIC
STOREY
i.e. ABOVE
CORNICE

KEYSTONE

ARCH

KEYSTONE

ENGAGED
COLUMN

BASE

DIE

PLINTH

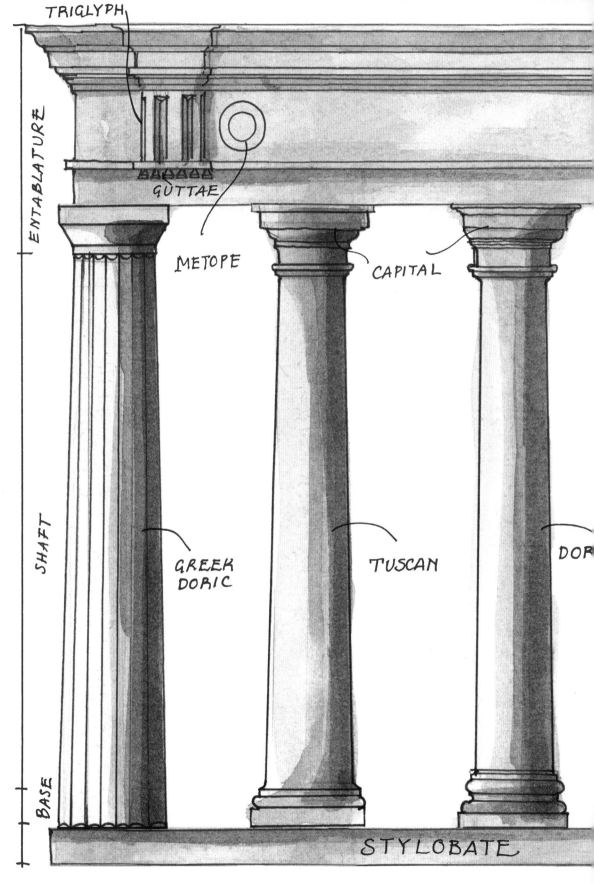

TRIGLYPH

ENTABLATURE

GUTTAE

METOPE

CAPITAL

SHAFT

GREEK
DORIC

TUSCAN

DOR

BASE

STYLOBATE

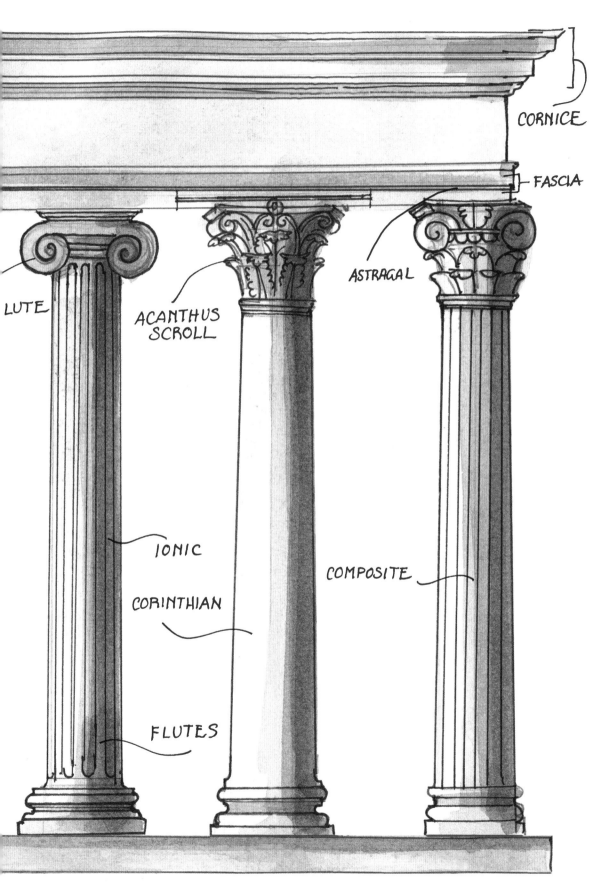

CORNICE

FASCIA

ASTRAGAL

LUTE

ACANTHUS
SCROLL

IONIC

COMPOSITE

CORINTHIAN

FLUTES

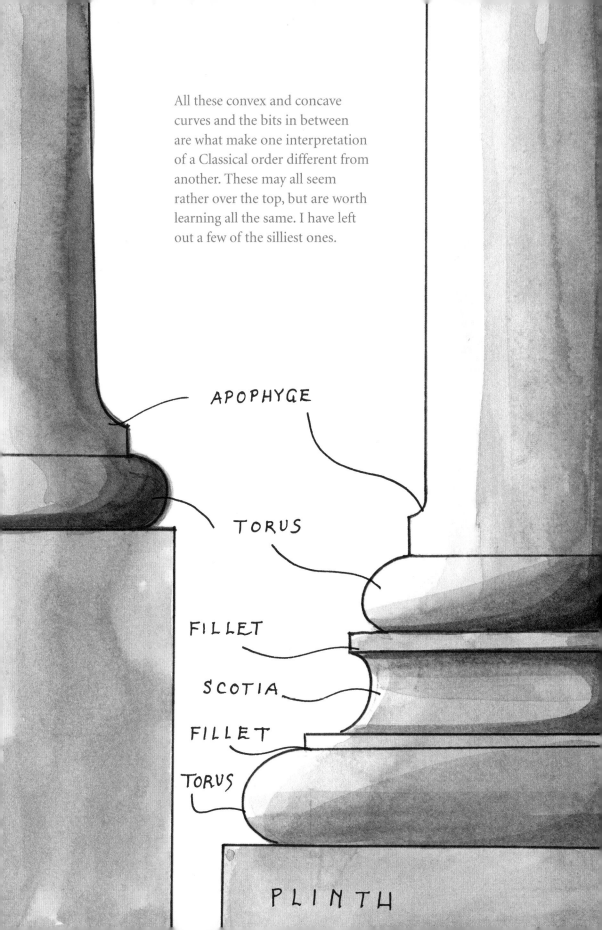

All these convex and concave curves and the bits in between are what make one interpretation of a Classical order different from another. These may all seem rather over the top, but are worth learning all the same. I have left out a few of the silliest ones.

APOPHYGE

TORUS

FILLET

SCOTIA

FILLET

TORUS

PLINTH

ABACUS

DART EGG BEAD & REEL

VOLUTE

FLUTE
FILLET

ABACUS

ECHINUS

FILLET

NECK

ASTRAGAL
FILLET

COLONNADE

FRIEZE

COUPLED COLUMNS

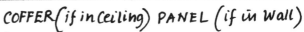
COFFER (if in ceiling) PANEL (if in wall)

PILASTER

ENGAGED COLUMN

COLUMN

The three illustrations on the left (drawn in plan, i.e. from above) show the relationships of column to building: pilaster (projecting only slightly from a wall), engaged column (attached or partly sunk into a wall) and freestanding column.

BALUSTRADE / RAIL   ✳ THESE ↑ are drawn in PLAN

RENAISSANCE BALUSTER

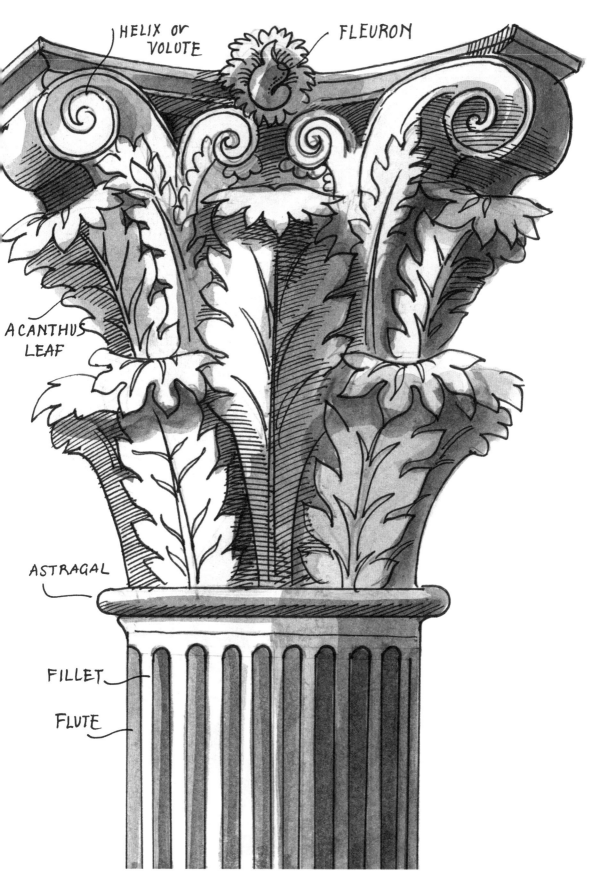

HELIX or VOLUTE

FLEURON

ACANTHUS LEAF

ASTRAGAL

FILLET

FLUTE

DOUBLE GREEK KEY

EGG & DART

GREEK KEY (or FRET)

BEAD & REEL

VITRUVIAN SCROLL

GUILLOCHE

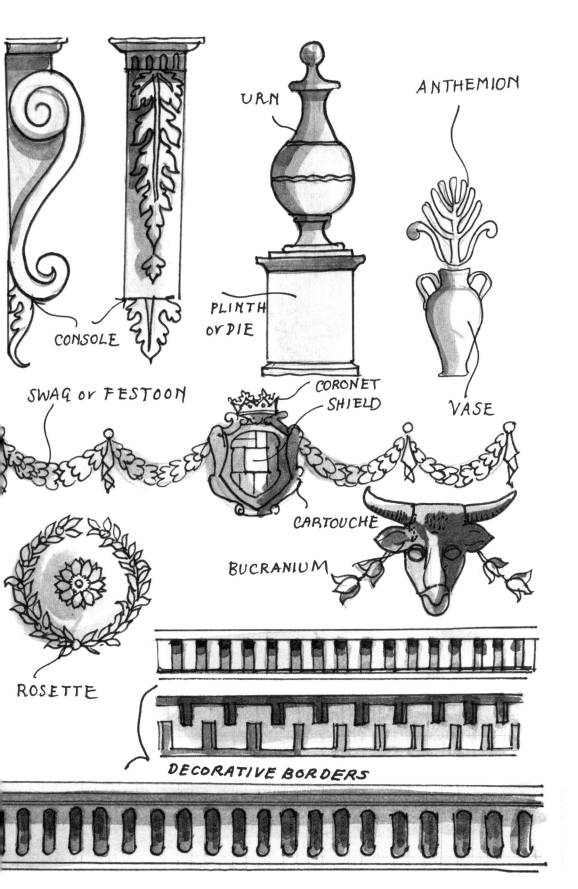

CONSOLE

URN

ANTHEMION

PLINTH or DIE

VASE

SWAG or FESTOON

CORONET
SHIELD

CARTOUCHE

ROSETTE

BUCRANIUM

DECORATIVE BORDERS

SADDLEBACK TOWER

BROACHED or SPLAYED foot TOWER

BROACH SPIRE

BROACH

GABLET

LUCARNE

CUPOLA

DOME

DRUM

ROUND TOWER

ST~WREN
TOWER

BATTLEMENTED
TOWER

NEEDLE
SPIRE

GEORGIAN TOWER
& CUPOLA

ROUND TOWER with
~ later OCTAGONAL TOP

These are some of the main towers, spires, domes and cupolas used in all buildings, Gothic or Classical. Church towers vary between regions.

There is a lot of nonsense said about round towers – that their shape is due to the stone available – but it is more likely that they are a style and nothing more.

A

VOCABVLARY

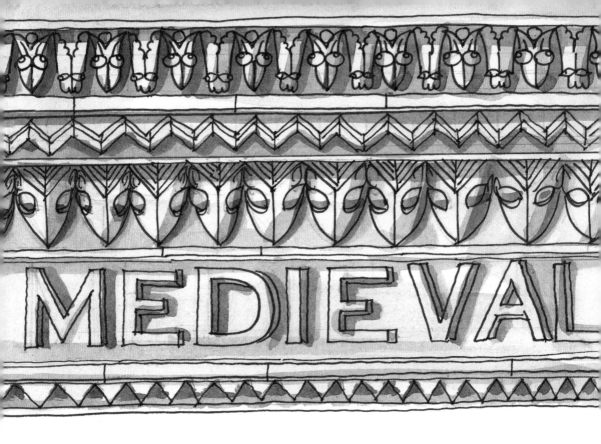

MEDIEVAL

The DARK AGES is the term used to describe the period between the end of Roman rule in Britain in AD450 and the century immediately before the Norman Conquest in 1066. Britain does not have a huge number of standing monuments left from those years. There are the Saxon churches, Brixworth and Earls Barton in Northamptonshire, Bradwell in Essex, Escomb in County Durham, Bradford-on-Avon in Wiltshire, and a handful of others. There are scraps of masonry incorporated into predominantly later buildings as well, such as at Dover Castle in Kent, but in general the score is low.

This is not, of course, to say that we had few buildings, even buildings of architectural merit. England, if not its Celtic fringes, was densely populated by standards of the period. The lack of surviving structures is simply a result of their being built of perishable wood. However, it is reasonable to assume that high-status buildings at this time would have been either ecclesiastical or defensive. Indeed, there was little change from this position until Henry VIII changed the entire social pattern of Britain when he dissolved the monasteries in the 1530s, at which point these properties came into private hands.

The adjective MUSCULAR is often used to describe NORMAN buildings. Certainly, this ex-Viking dynasty from northern France required terrific muscle to impose its rule on Britain. In an age without broadcasting or newspapers, the need for a method to disseminate the strength of the Norman invaders was met in part by its stone buildings. A regime capable of throwing up such impregnable and dominating defences as the White Tower in London or Dover Castle must have been overwhelmingly daunting to a potential Anglo-Saxon freedom fighter. The use of stone from the quarries of Caen in Normandy served to further emphasise this power.

The ROUND, ROMANESQUE or NORMAN arch is the key architectural component in Norman buildings. Although it was a relatively novel feature in England, this was a well-established tradition in mainland Europe that stretched back to ancient Rome. In the atomisation and general chaos following the sack and fall of Rome, the adoption of the city as an inspiration, whether architecturally, militarily or politically, was perceived as a way of assuming its mantle of authority and power. CHARLEMAGNE, ruler of the Franks from 768 to 814, was crowned Emperor of the Romans in 800, a title intended to override his position as a barbarian king. Thus the Romanesque arch, a component of the triumphal arches and, more significantly, of the arcading of Roman basilicas, became a politically and structurally significant component of the buildings of the CAROLINGIAN age. Two hundred years later it continued its imperial status as a symbol of the new aspirations of William of Normandy.

However, although the Romans had reserved their ornament for the capital of the column that supported the arch, the Normans decorated the arch itself. Dog's-tooth markings, stars and chevrons lined their arches in concentric semi-circles, producing the instantly recognisable Norman doorway.

The overall impression in Norman or Romanesque building is of martial strength. This is characterised by the use of massive walls, relatively small window openings, and strong, sometimes even rather squat, columns. Nor is this style reserved for military building: the great Norman CATHEDRALS are also robust. The early Norman bishops were a fairly warlike bunch – Odo, Bishop of Bayeux, later Earl of Kent, is featured on the Bayeux Tapestry wielding his mace with the best of them. His choice of weapon was due to canon law, which prevented him from lopping arms or heads with a sword like other knights. The bishops of Durham were PALATINATE BISHOPS, the equivalent of dukes, which meant they had the responsibility of maintaining law and order in their considerable northern territories, and even raising troops for their king. Later, in the fourteenth century, Henry Le Despenser, Bishop of Norwich, was pictured in full armour and, indeed, put down the Peasants' Revolt in 1381. The great churchmen of the early Middle Ages were no hair-shirted ascetics. They and their church were agents of Norman colonisation, and their churches were its visible manifestation. During the first hundred years of Norman rule thousands of churches were built of stone for the first time, thus taking the regime's values and its indubitable power directly into the Anglo-Saxon parishes of rural Britain.

Surviving domestic buildings are fewer, and it is only the largest that survive, usually because they are part of a monastic complex or defensive structure. One such is Castle Rising in Norfolk. This was built by WILLIAM D'ALBINI (c.1015–1061), another powerful Norman baron, and was a tremendous expression of his wealth. It remains a stonking and surprising building, its stair leading from outside to inside and through two intermediary doors to a wild *tour de force* of a Norman doorway. This dramatic arrival at a nobleman's front door reflects his importance in twelfth-century English society: D'Albini was married to the widow of Henry I and was a major regional magnate. Castle Rising uses the architectural language of the Norman church to trumpet the status of its owner. Small manors, such as Boothby Pagnell in Lincolnshire, are at least defendable, if not actual defensive, buildings. The siting of the private rooms on the first floor with storerooms beneath is indicative of a society not entirely at peace.

THOMAS RICKMAN (1776–1841) was an architectural historian whose study was the churches of the Middle Ages. He also became an architect, and designed many commissioners' Gothic churches of the early nineteenth century. It was he who coined the terms that we still use to differentiate the architectural styles of medieval churches: NORMAN, EARLY ENGLISH, DECORATED and PERPENDICULAR. The second two are the subject of the next chapter (page 46). He mapped important stylistic changes, the first of which was characterised by the abandonment of the Norman round arch and its replacement by the pointed or Gothic arch, which began in France in the middle of the twelfth century. It was not simply a matter of changing the arch, but was a totally new and more sophisticated system of building. The new Gothic cathedral or church was searching for LIGHT, so methods of increasing the number and size of openings became important. Windows became larger and were divided with PLATE TRACERY. Lightness was also achieved through construction – the heavy barrel vault or wooden ceiling was replaced with the groin and, later, lierne vaults. Contrasting colours of stone, particularly polished dark Purbeck marble, brought a greater visual articulacy to interiors, and piers now gave the impression of being made of clusters of slim attached shafts. The Gothic cathedral is a structure that feels like a skeleton in which one component bone supports the next, the stone walls, as the flesh, merely filling in the gaps.

Cathedrals were linked to monastic foundations, the dominating powers in medieval England. Abbeys and monasteries were hugely rich and initially of the BENEDICTINE order, many based architecturally on the prestigious house at Cluny in France. Later, in reaction to the lush worldliness of the Benedictines, the CISTERCIAN order was established. These ascetic monks established themselves in out-of-the-way (eventually perceived as Romantic) locations, such as Rievaulx and Tintern. The Benedictine Monastery was composed of gatehouse, church, cloister, abbot's lodging, chapter house, refectory, kitchen and dormitory, as well as various stores, privies and farm buildings. I have illustrated this arrangement, as it is frequently rather difficult to make out what was what when visiting an ex-monastic precinct today.

NOOK SHAFT

MOULDING or
STRING COURSE

INTERSECTING
BLIND ARCADING

PLINTH

GABLE

Castle Rising in Norfolk (1140) is a show-off Norman house, full of decoration and refined masonry. It reflects the high status of its builder, William D'Albini, who had recently married Henry I's widow. The carving is muscular and Romanesque, like that used in churches of the same period.

SHOULDERED WINDOWS

STRING COURSE

ROUND-TOPPED NORMAN WINDOW

CLASPING BUTTRESS

NOOK SHAFT

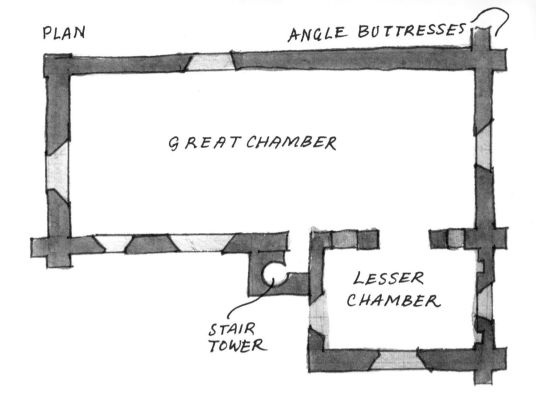

PLAN

GREAT CHAMBER

ANGLE BUTTRESSES

LESSER CHAMBER

STAIR TOWER

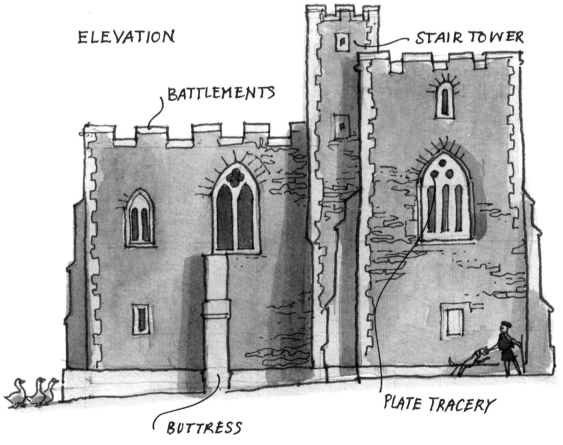

ELEVATION

STAIR TOWER

BATTLEMENTS

PLATE TRACERY

BUTTRESS

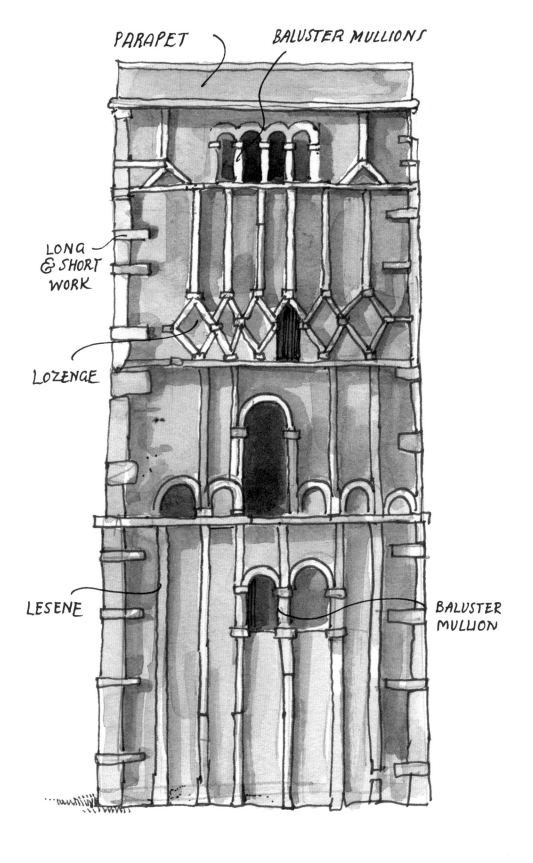

PARAPET

BALUSTER MULLIONS

LONG & SHORT WORK

LOZENGE

LESENE

BALUSTER MULLION

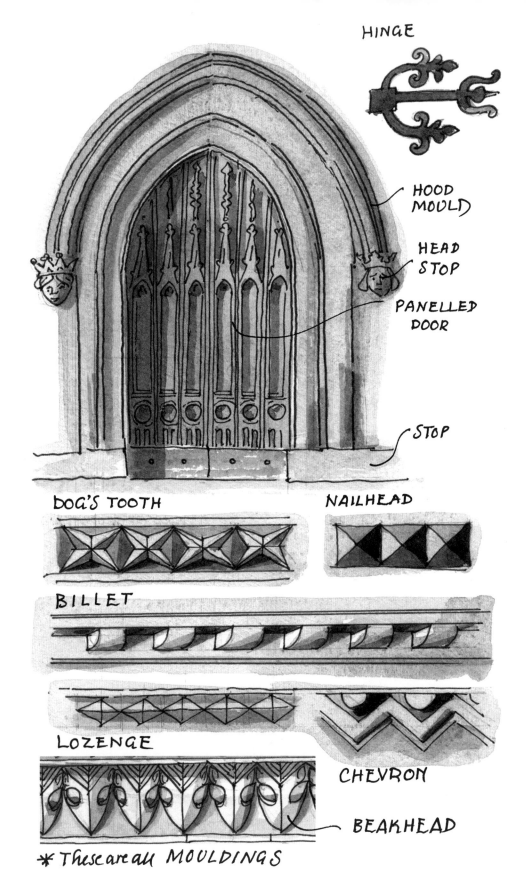

HINGE

HOOD MOULD

HEAD STOP

PANELLED DOOR

STOP

DOG'S TOOTH

NAILHEAD

BILLET

LOZENGE

CHEVRON

BEAKHEAD

* These are all MOULDINGS

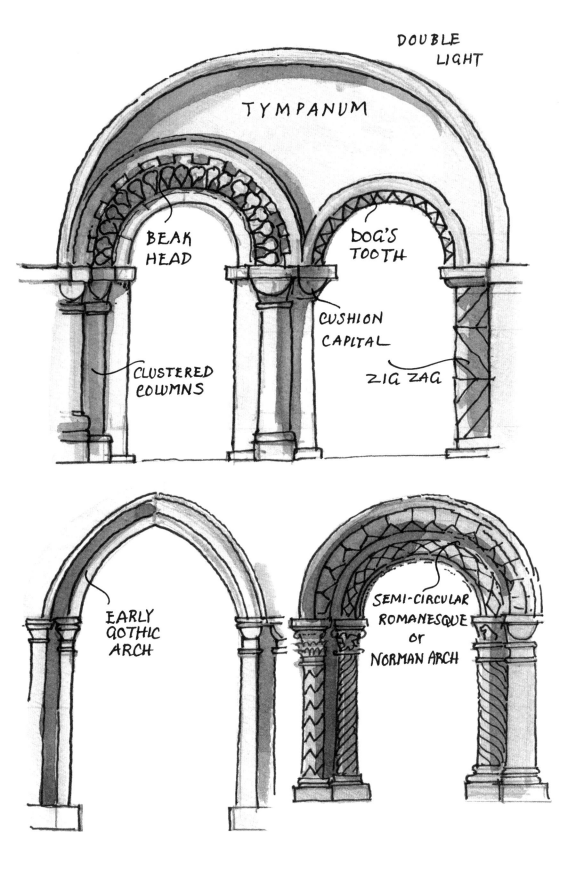

DOUBLE
LIGHT

TYMPANUM

BEAK
HEAD

DOG'S
TOOTH

CUSHION
CAPITAL

CLUSTERED
COLUMNS

ZIG ZAG

EARLY
GOTHIC
ARCH

SEMI-CIRCULAR
ROMANESQUE
OR
NORMAN ARCH

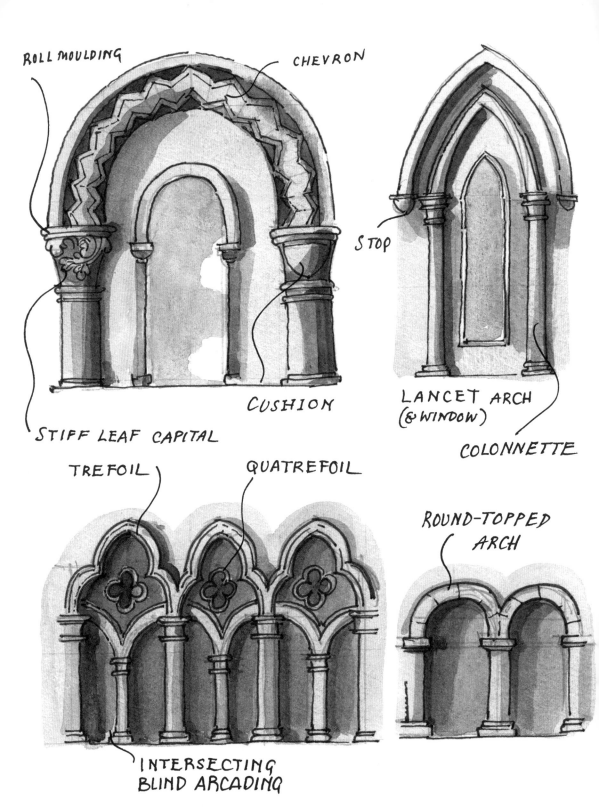

ROLL MOULDING

CHEVRON

STOP

CUSHION

LANCET ARCH
(& WINDOW)

STIFF LEAF CAPITAL

COLONNETTE

TREFOIL

QUATREFOIL

ROUND-TOPPED
ARCH

INTERSECTING
BLIND ARCADING

SAXON WINDOW

STILTED ARCH

BALUSTER MULLION

QUARRY (i.e. PANE)

HEAD STOP

PLATE TRACERY

Y TRACERY

INTERSECTING BLIND ARCADING

Early medieval windows are low on fripperies, all of which were yet to come. They were strong and muscular, with simple round-topped or pointed lancet arches, and the only divisions are 'plate' or 'Y tracery'. The pointed arch became popular in the late twelfth century.

COLLAR BEAM

BRACE

RAFTER

QUEEN POSTS

CRUCK BLADE

TIE BEAM

POST

GROIN VAULT
(*The GROIN is where the vaults meet*)

BARREL VAULT

QUADRIPARTITE RIBBED VAULT

MERLON

CRENEL (or EMBRASURE)

BATTLEMENTS or CRENELLATION

ARROW LOOP

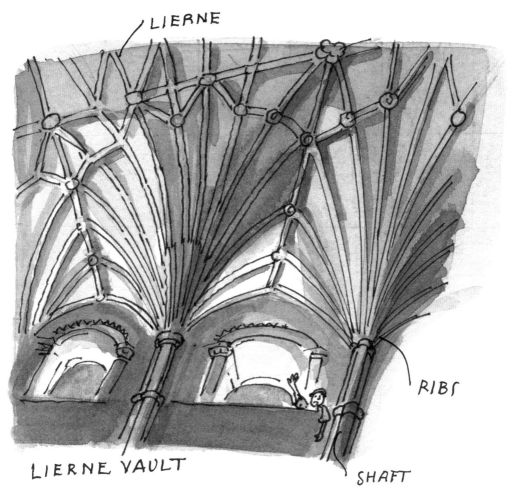

LIERNE

LIERNE VAULT

RIBS

SHAFT

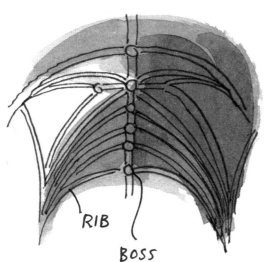

RIB

BOSS

Medieval builders were much concerned with the technical challenges presented by the roof. Vaulting, from simple barrel to later ribbed versions, is one of the triumphs of Gothic architecture, as are the elaborate timber roof structures. Battlements, later used as a shorthand for 'olde', are usually genuinely defensive at this time.

The DECORATED and PERPENDICULAR styles overlap, the former appearing first and merging with the latter. By the end of the thirteenth century, the first twinklings of decorated Gothic begin. Its origins are in the court style of France, and we see it first in Exeter, Ely, Lincoln and Wells Cathedrals and Westminster Abbey. Its features are many-ribbed VAULTS and arched windows with cursive and interlocking TRACERY, made up of cusping, daggers and mouchettes, trefoils and quatrefoils. The arches are wider at the base than their early English predecessors, sometimes called equilateral. The ogee arch, in which the arms swoop sinuously in to a peak, also appears now.

All these features combine in the Lady Chapel at Ely, begun in 1335. It is FULL OF LIGHT. The east window is a sheet of glass and, on each wall, above a row of ogival niches, are four more great decorated windows. The whole room is REFINED and SLENDER in detail.

It was completed in 1349, the year after the cataclysmic Black Death arrived in Britain, carried by the fleas on ships' rats. This disease, complete with horrid symptoms, killed between thirty and forty per cent of the population in the space of two years. That was bad, but in its aftermath came near economic disaster. England was a predominantly agricultural economy. A dire labour shortage, and the fact that whole villages had been wiped out, meant that much marginal land fell out of cultivation and wages began to spiral upwards. Canny landowners realised that, even with the most enthusiastic post-disaster population explosion, infant mortality and poverty would prevent the problem being alleviated. Therefore, they changed the emphasis of their farming from mixed to sheep. Sheep required far less manpower than mixed farming, and their wool and meat were cashcrops.

This change in agricultural practices had an equally dramatic economic effect, and the new wealth had an architectural manifestation: the great WOOL CHURCHES of East Anglia, the Cotswolds and the south-west. These were all built in the PERPENDICULAR style. Although the decorated and perpendicular schools overlap, they are very different in feeling. Gone was the effusive and sinuous curvilinear tracery that filled almost all the face of a window and the generous or cursive arch. Instead, the Perpendicular style's features are progressively shallower or depressed arches, windows with a minimum of transoms (horizontal crosspieces) and a more restrained area of tracery, shallow cusping and arching at the top of the window. Doorways, also with shallow arched tops, were surrounded in a rectangular frame. The space between the top of the arch and the edge of the frame, known as the spandrel, thus became a new area for decoration. BAY WINDOWS, known as oriel windows when suspended at an upper storey, developed at the end of the fourteenth century, and in the fifteenth century were much decorated with quatrefoils and blind arches. More importantly, they provided a sunny place to sit. Roofs became more and more intricate with the use of FAN VAULTING: inverted cones decorated with the finest ribbing. At their most elaborate, these had decorated pendants at their tips.

The changes in agriculture began a drift of populations to the towns, a process that was to continue for almost seven hundred years. Areas once farmed in strips by the whole village began to be consolidated into more private enclosures, which led to smaller numbers of less feudally dependant farmers. The countryside was further depopulated. THE BEGGARS WERE COMING TO TOWN.

The Black Death that swept through the population was not the only bad news. The year 1337 saw the beginning of a contest for the French throne between the English and the French that continued intermittently until 1453: THE HUNDRED YEARS WAR. In 1380, partly to raise funds for the war, John of Gaunt, as Regent for Richard II, levied a particularly unpopular tax, the Poll Tax, which dictated that every man over the age of fifteen should pay one shilling. Dissatisfaction led to the Peasants' Revolt in 1381.

This dire series of events also led to a gloomy obsession with the skeleton in art. In Dorchester, near Oxford, there is a fine pre-Black Death tomb. On it, the body of the knight lies asleep, yet poised to spring into action when he hears the final trumpet call. In the church at Ewelme, also in Oxfordshire, the more elaborate, later fifteenth-century tomb of Alice, Duchess of Suffolk, has her peaceful effigy on the top, but below, carved in alabaster, lies her decomposing body, with skeleton and scary skull clearly depicted.

HERALDRY also became increasingly important and visible in architecture. Coats of arms had first been used in the reign of Henry II (1133–89), but it was not until 1348 that Edward III established the Order of the Garter, the most important chivalric order in England. Late-medieval tombs and, indeed, porches and gatehouses, are often decorated with heraldic devices, carved, painted, rendered in stained glass or, in some of the great East Anglian churches, worked in knapped flint and contrasting limestone panels called FLUSHWORK. The spandrels of a doorway often bear the arms of the resident or donor family, as do bosses or stained-glass panels in windows.

Although churches were thriving in the late Middle Ages, the manor house and other secular buildings were only just coming into their own. The CASTLE, which in Norman times was an expression of brute strength, began to relax, and to supply the varied and less-defensive needs of a more established nobility. John of Gaunt began rebuilding Kenilworth Castle in Warwickshire in 1392. His splendid GREAT HALL was 90ft long and 45ft wide, nearly as large as the entire Norman keep. The windows are graceful and tall, with elegant cusping and tracery. The plan was that of all medieval halls: it was raised on a vaulted undercroft, and was entered by a stair and a door that led to the screens. These divided the hall from the service rooms, the buttery, pantry and servants' quarters. But although this room, now in ruins, must have been as grand as any that would follow for two hundred years, it was not built to a symmetrical plan of the sort that would be adopted later, but as one of a series of buildings irregularly arranged around a COURTYARD. Courtyards had the advantage of letting more LIGHT into rooms in an age when artificial lighting was a luxury. For reasons of safety, kitchens were often separate buildings altogether, and were huge. Those of Stanton Harcourt (1470) and Glastonbury Abbey (1400) are 25ft and 34ft long respectively, and their octagonal roofs rise to 40ft high. These are unusual in surviving and became the models for nineteenth-century reproductions, for example, the Museum of Natural History at Oxford or Tyntesfield near Bristol.

GATEHOUSES became an important building type. These were more than just lodges. They were the entrance to a house, secular or monastic, that was arranged in a series of courtyards. Earlier structures might contain a guard room and serve as a miniature castle, but, increasingly, they were to become more domestic, built to accommodate visitors or to store records. These gatehouses were to assume more architectural importance under the reign of the Tudors.

INFILL or NOGGING

JETTY

QUOIN

BUTTRESS

PLINTH

TWO-LIGHT WINDOW

SHIELD in SPANDRE

RIDGE

BRACE

STUD

STUD

STUD
(STUDDING)

BRESSUMER

The George Inn in Norton St Philip, Somerset, licensed in 1397, may be the oldest pub still in use. The ground floor is late fourteenth century, but the wooden super-stucture is fifteenth century. It owes its grandness to the wool fair of the town, which ran from the fourteenth century until the final fleece was sold in 1902.

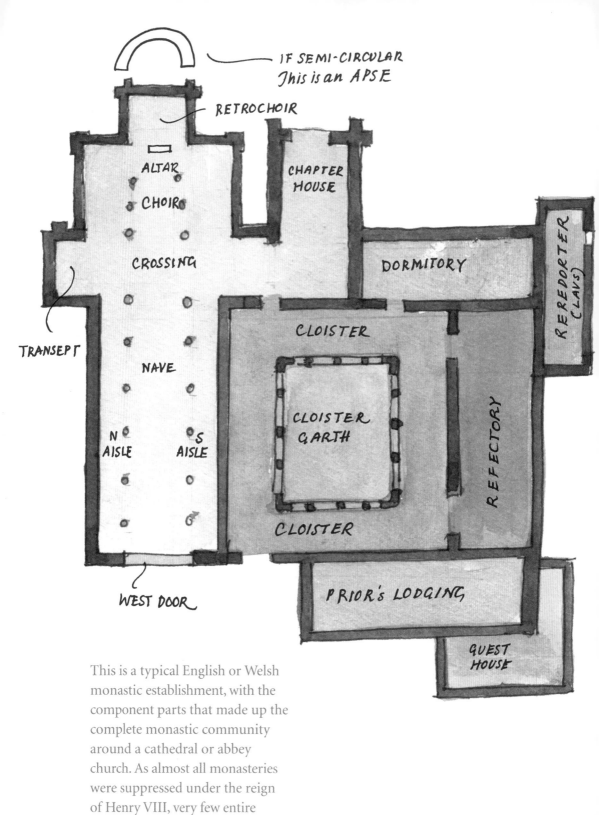

IF SEMI-CIRCULAR
This is an APSE

RETROCHOIR

ALTAR

CHOIR

CHAPTER HOUSE

CROSSING

DORMITORY

REREDORTER (LAVS)

TRANSEPT

NAVE

CLOISTER

CLOISTER GARTH

N AISLE

S AISLE

REFECTORY

CLOISTER

WEST DOOR

PRIOR'S LODGING

GUEST HOUSE

This is a typical English or Welsh monastic establishment, with the component parts that made up the complete monastic community around a cathedral or abbey church. As almost all monasteries were suppressed under the reign of Henry VIII, very few entire complexes have survived.

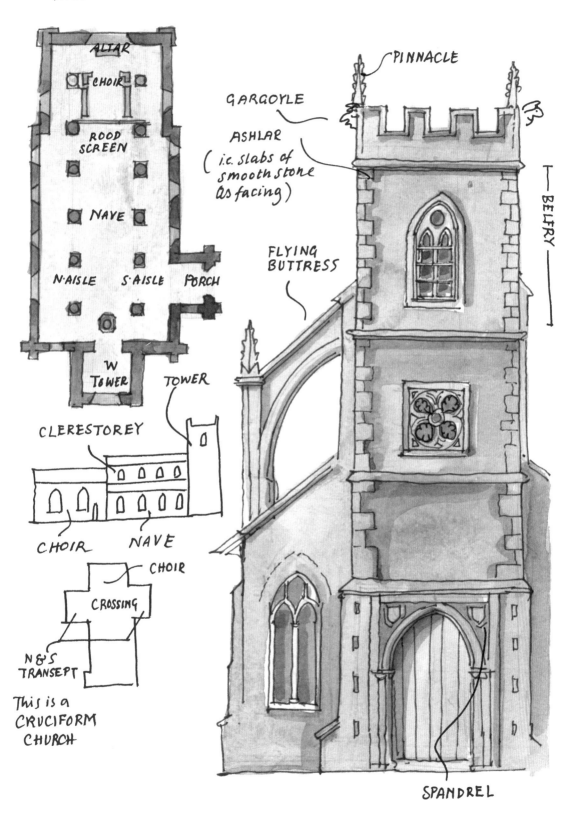

GROUND PLAN

ALTAR

CHOIR

ROOD SCREEN

NAVE

N·AISLE   S·AISLE   PORCH

W TOWER

PINNACLE

GARGOYLE

ASHLAR
(i.e. slabs of smooth stone as facing)

FLYING BUTTRESS

BELFRY

TOWER

CLERESTOREY

CHOIR   NAVE

CHOIR

CROSSING

N & S TRANSEPT

This is a CRUCIFORM CHURCH

SPANDREL

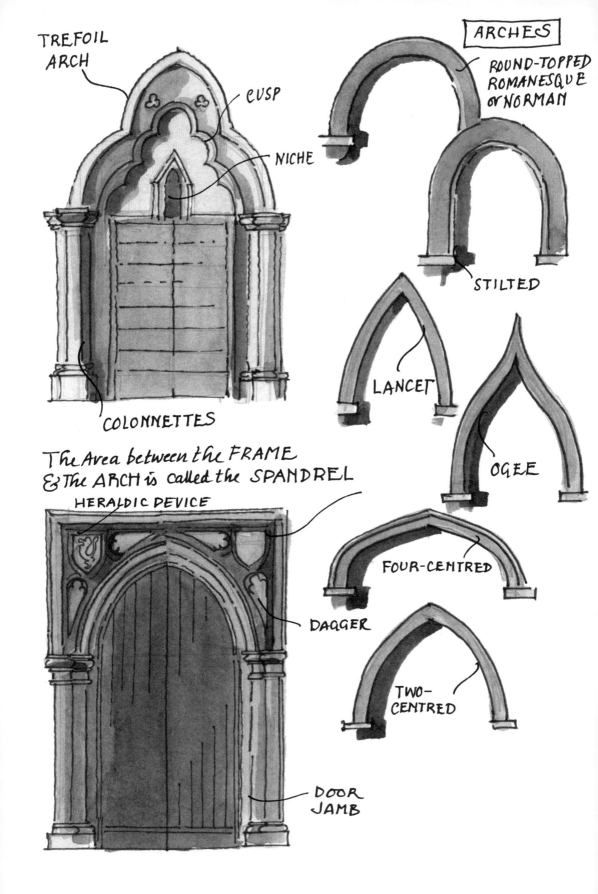

TREFOIL ARCH

CUSP

NICHE

COLONNETTES

The Area between the FRAME & the ARCH is called the SPANDREL

HERALDIC DEVICE

DAGGER

DOOR JAMB

ARCHES

ROUND-TOPPED ROMANESQUE or NORMAN

STILTED

LANCET

OGEE

FOUR-CENTRED

TWO-CENTRED

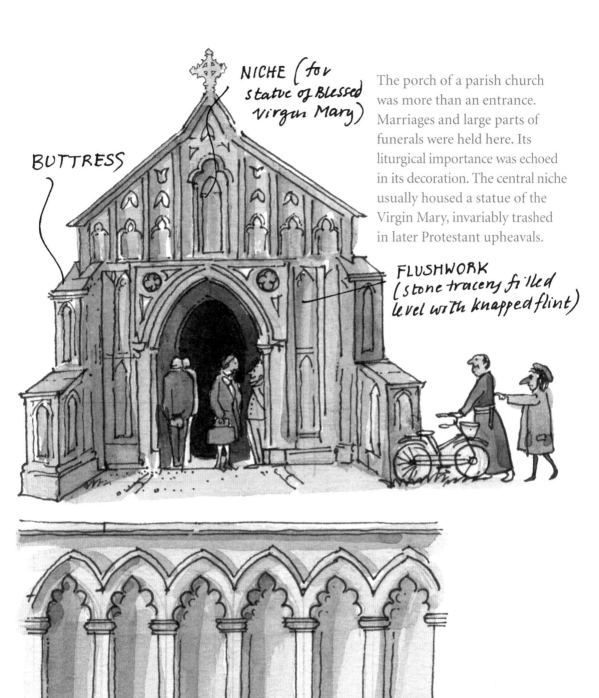

NICHE (for statue of Blessed Virgin Mary)

BUTTRESS

The porch of a parish church was more than an entrance. Marriages and large parts of funerals were held here. Its liturgical importance was echoed in its decoration. The central niche usually housed a statue of the Virgin Mary, invariably trashed in later Protestant upheavals.

FLUSHWORK (stone tracery filled level with knapped flint)

BLIND ARCADE

ORIEL WINDOW
(It sticks out but does <u>not</u> go to the ground)

MOUCHETTE (Curved)

DAGGER (straight)

PANELLING

CORBEL

HOOD MOULD

CUSPED ARCHES

PERPENDICULAR TRACERY

TRANSOM

DECORATED TRACERY

FINIAL

CROCKETING

PANELLING

CROCKETS

OGEE

...GGER

...ST

...D
...OP

MULLION

PERPENDICULAR TRACERY

MULLION

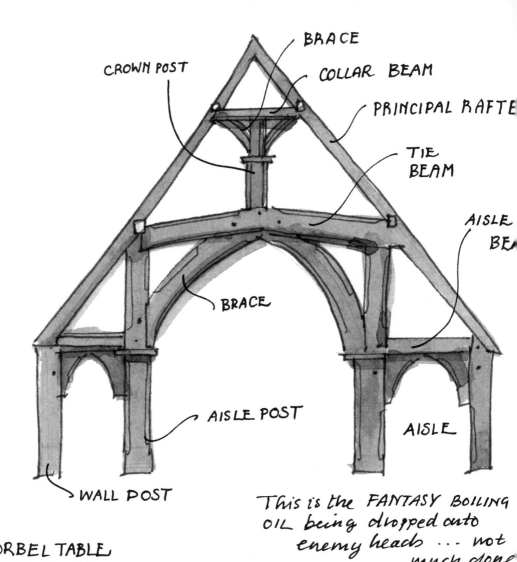

CROWN POST

BRACE

COLLAR BEAM

PRINCIPAL RAFTE

TIE BEAM

AISLE BE

BRACE

AISLE POST

AISLE

WALL POST

CORBEL TABLE

This is the FANTASY BOILING OIL being dropped onto enemy heads ... not much done sadly

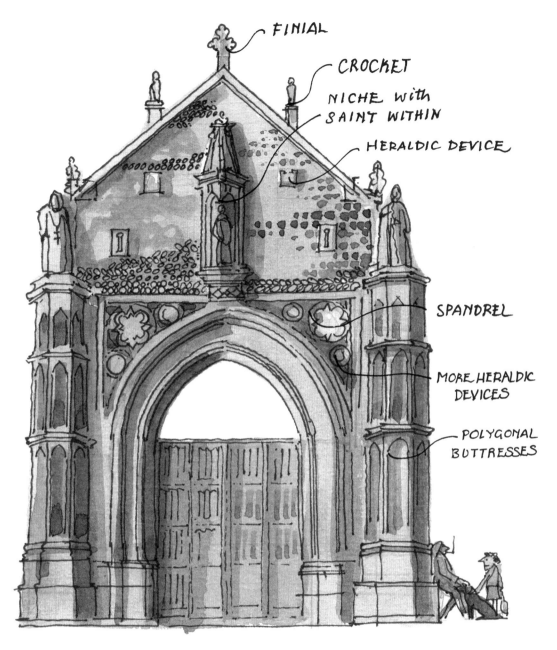

FINIAL

CROCKET

NICHE WITH SAINT WITHIN

HERALDIC DEVICE

SPANDREL

MORE HERALDIC DEVICES

POLYGONAL BUTTRESSES

This is the Erpingham Gate at Norwich Cathedral. The setting of the archway within a rectangular frame is characteristic of late medieval architecture, as is the panelling of the turrets. The niche containing the saint was originally intended to house a statue of the donor: the hero of Agincourt, Sir Thomas Erpingham.

CUSPING i.e.

PILLAR

TUDOR & ELIZABETHAN

The Tudor dynasty began with victory at the Battle of Bosworth Field in 1485 and ended with the death of Elizabeth I in 1603. This long period saw a great change in the buildings of what was fast becoming Britain rather than England. The most architecturally significant event was the BREAK WITH ROME, the culmination of Henry VIII's struggle with the Pope. The pontiff's unwillingness to accede to Henry's desire to see his marriage to Catherine of Aragon annulled had significant consequences for the buildings of his realm.

The RENAISSANCE had been in full swing in Italy for a hundred years. FILIPPO BRUNELLESCHI (1377–1446) and LEONE ALBERTI (1404–72) were the great architects who had interpreted the ruins of ancient Rome. In the highly evolved Classical ORDERS and in the first-century-AD writing of MARCUS VITRUVIUS, they had seen the pattern for a new architecture. Then, in the early sixteenth century, the full glories of the late Renaissance flowered in Italy. Italian architects were working all over Europe disseminating these new ideas, but there was an understandable resistance to all things Italian in the English court and a reluctance for any Italian architect of the first rank to work in England. This led to a CULTURAL ISOLATION in terms of architecture that lasted until James I employed Inigo Jones in 1610.

This does not mean that the Renaissance did not touch England. In 1563, JOHN SHUTE, who had been sent to Europe in 1550 by his patron, the Duke of Northumberland, published *The First and Chief Groundes of Architecture*. He had seen the work of the Italian architects and studied the work of SEBASTIANO SERLIO (1475–1554), who had published his five influential *Books of Architecture* between 1537 and 1547. These, together with other publications, mainly from the Netherlands, illustrated examples of Classical ornament. Although the underlying laws of Classical architecture were not yet understood, or at any rate not adopted, there was a great appetite for the decorative elements within it. Columns, capitals, pediments and cornices appeared everywhere, particularly on church monuments and tombs, and as components in the design of doorways and gatehouses.

Significantly, Shute describes himself as 'paynter and Archytecte'. This was an important moment, marking the beginning of a new profession. Before then, there had been masons and surveyors, but not architects. ROBERT SMYTHSON (c.1536–1614), who designed Wollaton and Longleat, also styled himself 'Gent, Architector and Surveyor'. There had been architectural drawings before, but it is from this date onwards that elevations and plans or PLATS survive.

The cultural isolation of England was not the only consequence of the break with Rome. Equally significant was the change in land ownership that the Dissolution of the Monasteries implied. At the beginning of Henry VIII's reign, there were more than eight hundred RELIGIOUS HOUSES: Benedictines, Cistercians, Franciscans and many other smaller orders. Monasteries, nunneries and the open orders of friars who worked in the wider community all combined to exert considerable power. Importantly, they also owned a third of the land. The houses were so well dispersed that you were never further than half an hour's walk from one in England, and perhaps an hour in Wales. At the Dissolution, the properties passed to the Crown, whose agents sold them as quickly as possible. The most likely purchasers were local gentry and nobility, who were able to add to their estates or were, in effect, forced to do so in order to maintain status. The buildings themselves, usually unroofed by the commissioners to prevent the dispersed monkish communities from reconvening, were sometimes sold, usually for materials, or utilised by local people as quarries. The roofless walls were plundered for chunks of stone, and even complete windows and doorways. Consequently, MONASTIC FRAGMENTS of this sort often turn up in secular buildings.

As I mentioned in the last chapter, the GOTHIC style continued until the very eve of the Dissolution. Henry VII's chapel at Westminster Abbey was completed in 1520 (after his death), and the extraordinary fan-vaulted ceiling of King's College Chapel, Cambridge, dates from 1530. However, the REFORMATION did have a dramatic effect on church building in England and Wales. Most notable in plan was the reduction of the CHANCEL, both in importance and physical size. This reflected the change of emphasis in Christian worship from the EUCHARIST, celebrated at the east end, to the preaching of the SERMON, which took place in the pulpit. Some chancels were removed altogether and a wall built across the chancel arch. In cases where a window was reintroduced, it was one of great austerity, sometimes so Perpendicular that it had no tracery at all. Binham Priory in Norfolk effectively illustrates these changes. This former Benedictine priory was founded in 1091 by a nephew of William the Conqueror, who endowed it with the Manor of Binham. It was dissolved in 1539 and sold to Thomas Paston. Everything was destroyed, dispersed or fell into disrepair, except the main part of the nave, which was retained by the new CHURCH OF ENGLAND as a parish church, the new east wall (built where the rood screen originally sat) having an entirely rectangular window fitted. At least one house, in the High Street of Wells-next-the-Sea, is recorded as being built of salvaged masonry from the priory.

With the exception of Henry VIII, the Tudor monarchs were not great builders. His major surviving creations are the magnificent extension to Wolsey's palace at Hampton Court and the vast palace at Nonsuch. His children were not builders, and it was not until the coming of the STUARTS that the Court led in the field of architecture.

As previously stated, the focus of architectural effort since the Conquest had been defensive or ecclesiastical. Secular domestic buildings were of course produced, but their non-survival is testament to their lesser importance. In the sixteenth century, minor landowners, through consolidation of holdings or lucrative offices, or indeed from the acquisition of former monastic lands, became richer, and deserted their old manor houses in favour of smarter models, better fitted to their enhanced position. Manors that became irrelevant due to these changes were relegated to farmhouse status or fell into disrepair.

Great houses were also being built, not only by old territorial magnates, but by the new men at Court. William Cecil – Lord Burghley – built Burghley House from 1555 to 1587, Sir John Thynne built Longleat from 1570 to 1580, and Sir Francis Willoughby built Wollaton from 1580 to 1588. These PRODIGY HOUSES used the new CLASSICAL VOCABULARY, but they spoke the language stiltingly and, in some cases, clumsily. An extraordinary example is Hardwick Hall, built by Bess of Hardwick, the Countess of Shrewsbury, between 1590 and 1597, to designs by Smythson. Dubbed 'Hardwick Hall, more glass than wall', the house has unusually tall windows on the second floor, lighting the state apartments. On the ground floor is a loggia supported by eight Tuscan pillars that runs across the central six bays. Particularly characteristic of great houses of this period is the pierced parapet composed of stone scrolls, coronets and the owner's initials, ES, crowning the four towers. Although this is not really a Classical building, the cornice that divides the storeys definitely IS Classical, not Gothic, as the pillars on the loggia and balusters are. Also, SYMMETRY in plan was increasingly adopted in large houses, yet another sign of the Renaissance permeating the style of buildings.

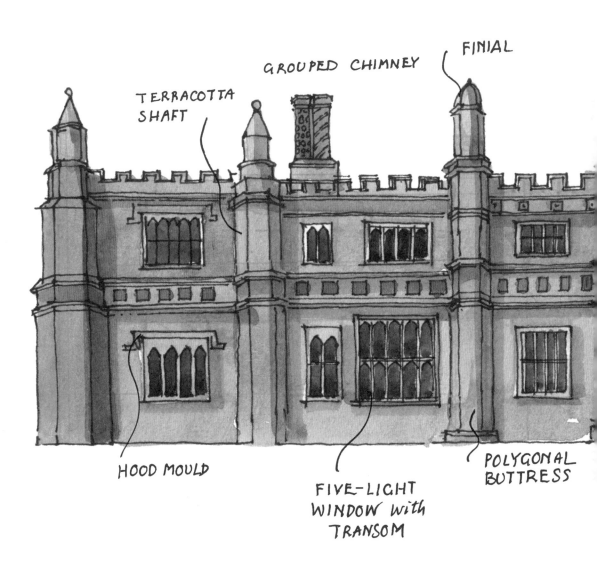

GROUPED CHIMNEY

FINIAL

TERRACOTTA SHAFT

HOOD MOULD

FIVE-LIGHT WINDOW with TRANSOM

POLYGONAL BUTTRESS

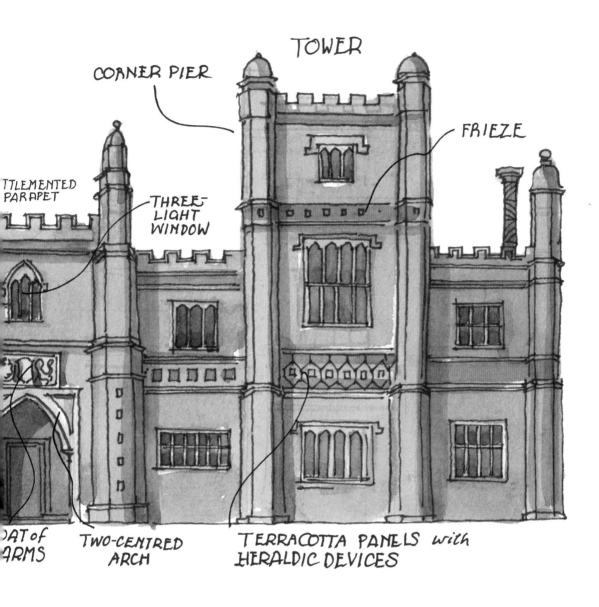

TOWER

CORNER PIER

FRIEZE

TTLEMENTED
PARAPET

THREE-
LIGHT
WINDOW

OAT of
ARMS

TWO-CENTRED
ARCH

TERRACOTTA PANELS with
HERALDIC DEVICES

East Barsham Manor in Norfolk (1520) is exceptionally grand. Its red brick is liberally scattered with terracotta decoration, shields and medallions, like those at Hampton Court.

Significant brick building in Britain is first seen in East Anglia and London because of their close trading links with the Low Countries, where brick had long been employed.

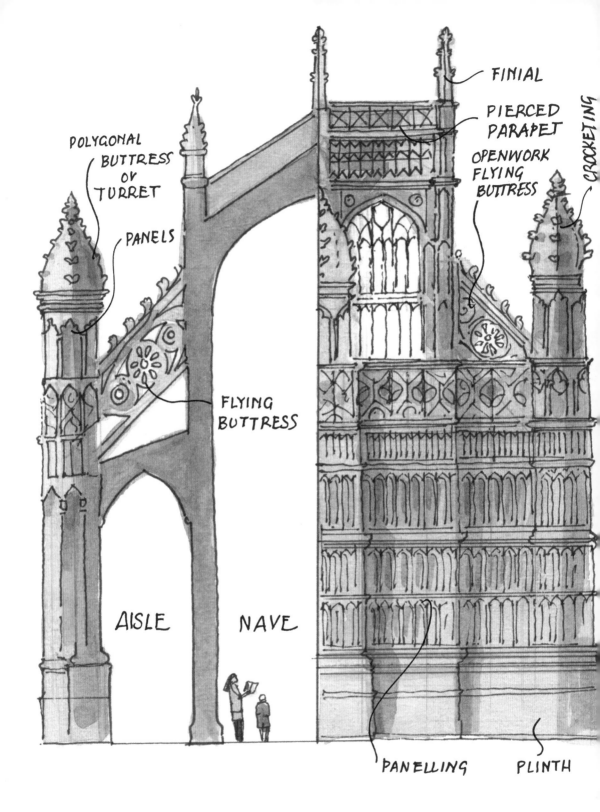

FINIAL

PIERCED PARAPET

OPENWORK FLYING BUTTRESS

CROCKETING

POLYGONAL BUTTRESS or TURRET

PANELS

FLYING BUTTRESS

AISLE

NAVE

PANELLING

PLINTH

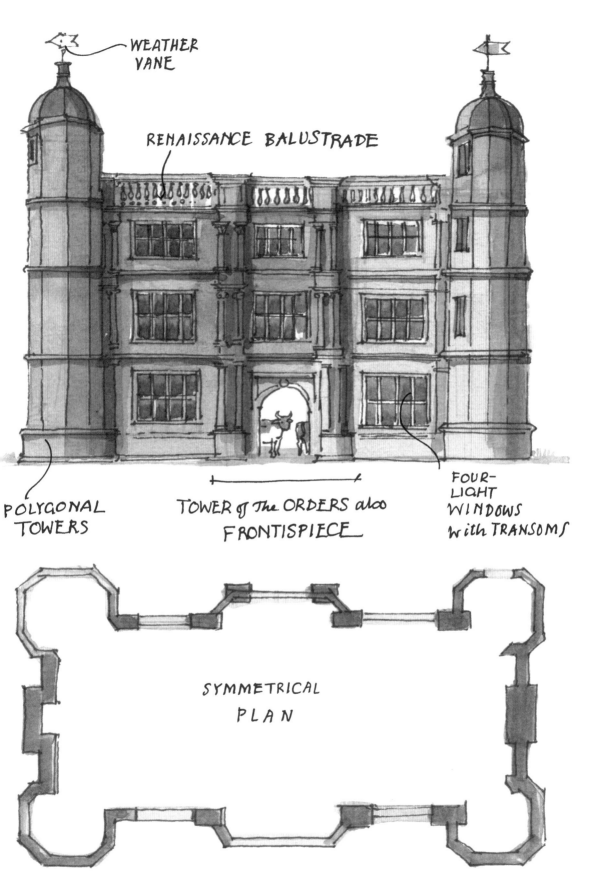

WEATHER VANE

RENAISSANCE BALUSTRADE

POLYGONAL TOWERS

TOWER of The ORDERS also FRONTISPIECE

FOUR-LIGHT WINDOWS with TRANSOMS

SYMMETRICAL PLAN

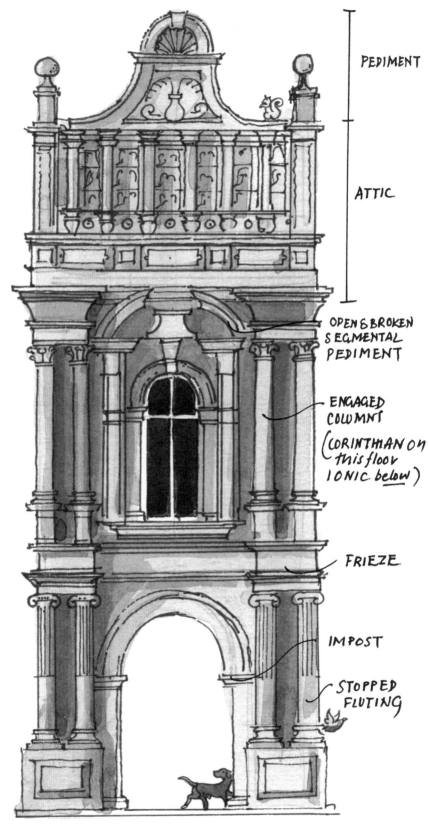

PEDIMENT

ATTIC

OPEN & BROKEN
SEGMENTAL
PEDIMENT

ENGAGED
COLUMNS
(CORINTHIAN on
this floor
IONIC below)

FRIEZE

IMPOST

STOPPED
FLUTING

FRONTISPIECE OR TOWER OF THE ORDERS

BRICK VOUSSOIRS

FOUR-CENTRED ARCH

HOOD MOULD

STOP

ARCHITRAVE   PLINTH

CORNICE

FRIEZE

ARCHITRAVE

...NIC
...PITAL

...UTING

...ILLED
...TING

...ed
...DING

...E

Here are the first glimmerings of Classicism coming to Britain. This gateway (left) at Bolsover in Derbyshire has fine Ionic columns, but is rather over-decorated. Opposite is a frontispiece with Classical elements arranged in a fairly convincing fashion, but the top storey is still a bit odd.

This whole thing,
the doorway & its
surround, is an
AEDICULE

MERLON

BATTLEMENTED PARAPET

These windows show
the final gasp of Gothic
detail, and the enthusiastic,
if untutored, adoption of
Classical ornament.

BAY or
DAIS WINDOW (i.e.
the Dais in the Hall
is behind it. inside)

MULLION

BAR

TRANSOM

BRICK
KEYSTONE

SEGMENTAL
PEDIMENT

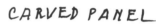

CARVED PANEL

— AGAIN, This whole thing
is an AEDICULE

— APRON

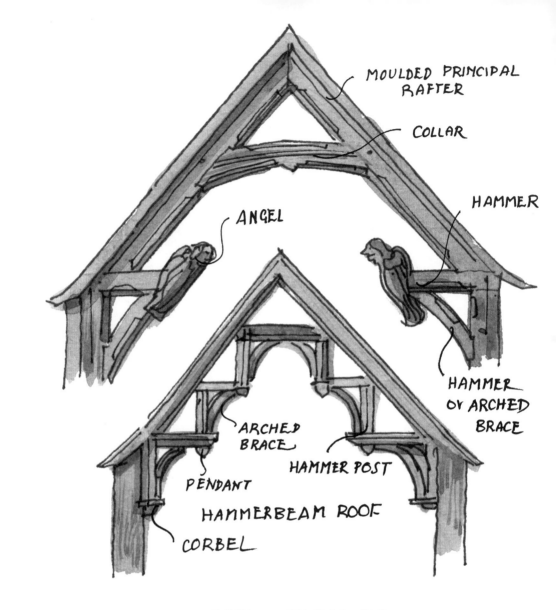

MOULDED PRINCIPAL RAFTER

COLLAR

HAMMER

ANGEL

HAMMER OV ARCHED BRACE

ARCHED BRACE

HAMMER POST

PENDANT

HAMMERBEAM ROOF

CORBEL

OPENWORK BALUSTRADE

URN

RAIL

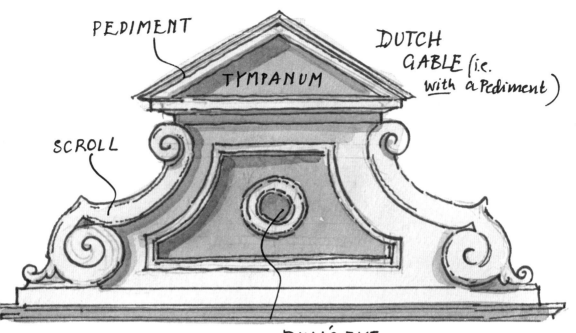

PEDIMENT

TYMPANUM

DUTCH GABLE (i.e. with a Pediment)

SCROLL

BULL'S EYE or OEIL-de-BOEUF

SHAPED GABLE (i.e. with NO Pediment)

PINNACLE

THREE-LIGHT WINDOW

The openwork balustrade with urns (opposite) is a good late-Elizabethan detail. This, and all similar strapwork, would be swept away by the next century's Classicism. The shaped gables (above) came from Holland, so they are sometimes called Dutch Gables, although, to be strictly accurate, they should have a pediment atop to be Dutch.

When James VI of Scotland arrived to be king of England in 1603, he found a very inward-looking country. With few foreign outposts, England's minor trading arrangements were dwarfed by the more established Spanish and Portuguese empires. The country's view of mainland Europe was focused on Spanish aggression and French antagonism. A healthy mistrust of cross-Channel friendship and travel had, as discussed, insulated England from the cultural explosion of the RENAISSANCE. But Scotland's links with Europe, in particular with France, the AULD ALLIANCE, were strong, and James's ascension to the throne (as James I of England) overturned, in part, the long-standing insularity of England.

However, some ideas had already made their way across the Channel and were filtering into English architecture. In Nuremberg in 1598, Wendel Dietterlin (1550–99) had published an architectural treatise that was based on the work of Vitruvius, but which was written with an alarming FREEDOM OF INTERPRETATION. Vredeman de

Vries (1527–1606) had done something similar in the Netherlands. The evidence of their influence in England was first apparent in ELIZABETHAN buildings. Longleat, Wollaton and Hardwick were all built in the second half of the sixteenth century, and were beginning to make use of CLASSICAL ORNAMENT as applied decoration.

Blickling in Norfolk, with its forest of chimneys and Dutch gables, and the great palace of Audley End in Essex are powerful examples of Classicism developing in the sixteenth century. Then, at the beginning of the seventeenth century, buildings such as Bolsover Castle (begun in 1612), the work of Robert and John Smythson, showed details from the engravings of Dietterlin and de Vries employed in stone. These were the further glimmerings of an understanding of the actual SYSTEM OF CLASSICISM, of how one column relates to another and to the ENTABLATURE, comprising an architrave, frieze and cornice, that sits on top of them. This use of the ancient temple or triumphal arch form had begun with the Gate of Honour (1557) of Gonville & Caius College, Cambridge. However, with their massive stone mullions and oriels, and with their SKYLINES still dominated by chimneyscapes, shaped gables, battlements and openwork parapets with lettering, these magnificent houses were the last gasp of the OLD WAYS.

Meanwhile, the artist, designer, architect, producer of masques at Court and general polymath INIGO JONES (1573–1652) went to Italy between 1597 and 1603. He travelled from Florence and Rome to Venice, where he studied the work of the high priest of CLASSICISM, the architect ANDREA PALLADIO (1508–80). Palladio was working in a revolutionary new way with the Classical orders. Through his study of the ANTIQUE, the ruins of ancient Rome, he was creating a new architecture. His powerful clients, the rich ruling families of Venice and the Veneto, competed for ascendancy through the medium of architecture by commissioning more and more advanced buildings: the BASILICA in Vicenza and the CHURCHES of San Giorgio Maggiore (1564–80), the Redentore (1576) and the Zitelle (1581–88). These were all public buildings, but outside the city, along the Brenta Canal and in the rest of the inland Venetian empire, those same noble families who had commissioned the young architect's work in Venice had been building outstandingly modern VILLAS as summer houses and grand centrepieces of their innovative model agricultural estates, such as the Rotonda and the Villa Pisani. This interest in agriculture was a result of the downturn in the maritime fortunes of the Venetian Republic and the Venetians' realisation that they would have to turn, in part, to their *terra firma* territories for a new source of income.

The breathless excitement of this late-Renaissance outpouring left Jones inspired. He returned to the Court of James I ready to work in the new style. However, this pared-down and intellectually rigorous PALLADIANISM was at odds with the heavily decorated Jacobean orthodoxy, and Jones's first great work, the QUEEN'S HOUSE (1616–18) in Greenwich, must have seemed as odd as the Lloyd's building being erected in the middle of Ludlow. Cool, calculated resolutions and austere use of ornament produced at Greenwich something completely new. The gateway he designed for Beaufort House in Chelsea (now at Chiswick House) was as pure an imitation of the architecture of the ancients as existed in northern Europe, and very different from any contemporary usage of Classical style.

Jones continued to build, but his work was split between architecture and his other fields of interest as James I continued to order grander and yet grander masques. In 1622, Jones completed his greatest work, the BANQUETING HOUSE in Whitehall. This was designed as part of a larger replanning of the whole Royal Palace of Whitehall, up until then a mish-mash of a medieval palace. Jones had already redesigned the Star Chamber, but, in 1619, a fire destroyed nearly the whole area. The Banqueting House was the first part of what might have been a complete Inigo Jones Whitehall, but funds were short and even the drawings for it were not produced until 1638.

The Banqueting House is composed of a rusticated ground floor, with what appears from the outside to be two more storeys, but which is revealed on the inside to be one double-height room.

It is in the form of a simplified BASILICA, or nave of a church, and originally had a niche or apse at one end that would have made the basilica form more clear. It must have seemed utterly extraordinary to any Englishman who had NOT travelled to Italy and who knew only the great rooms of Hatfield and Burghley, although to those who had visited Vicenza or Venice it would surely have been familiar. The room at first-floor level was described by Colen Campbell in his introduction to *Vitruvius Britannicus* as 'without dispute, the first room in the world' – no small boast writing a hundred years later when the taste for Palladianism had at last caught on.

At the same time, Jones was working on the Prince's Lodging at Newmarket, a building now lost and recorded only in drawings. The Lodging would have been seen as the model for hundreds of Classical country houses for the next two hundred years. As it is, Jones's work is frustratingly thin on the ground.

These were the two opposing forces in early seventeenth-century British architecture. One, the heavily decorated style of Blickling and Audley End, was really the last reprise of the OLD ORDER of medieval and Tudor England. Although Gothic survived, slinking surreptitiously along throughout the seventeenth century in churches and Oxford and Cambridge colleges, the great ENGLISH RENAISSANCE would not resurface for 250 years, when the Victorians used it to define the architecture of Imperial Britain as a world power, evoking a revival of Good Queen Bess's reign in houses such as Harlaxton and Eynsham Hall.

However, the Palladianism of Jones and Nicholas Stone (1586–1647), master mason to James I from 1626, was the vanguard of the NEW STYLE, the CLASSICISM that would remain the dominant style until the 1840s. It varied and developed through several generations of architects, but always looked back with admiration at its father, Jones. Even after the Gothic Revival of the mid-nineteenth century, Classicism remained beside the neo-Gothic, Tudorbethan and Italianate/neo-Byzantine movements, outlasting them into the twentieth century and on into our own.

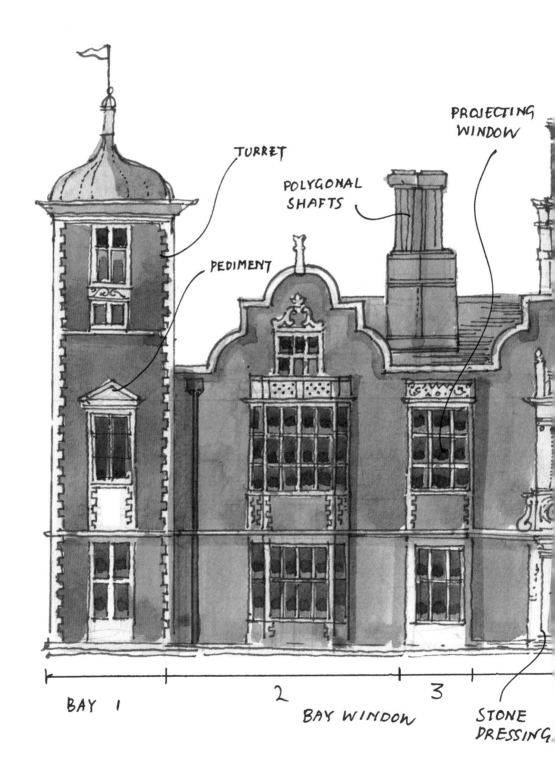

PROJECTING
WINDOW

TURRET

POLYGONAL
SHAFTS

PEDIMENT

BAY 1

2

BAY WINDOW

3

STONE
DRESSING

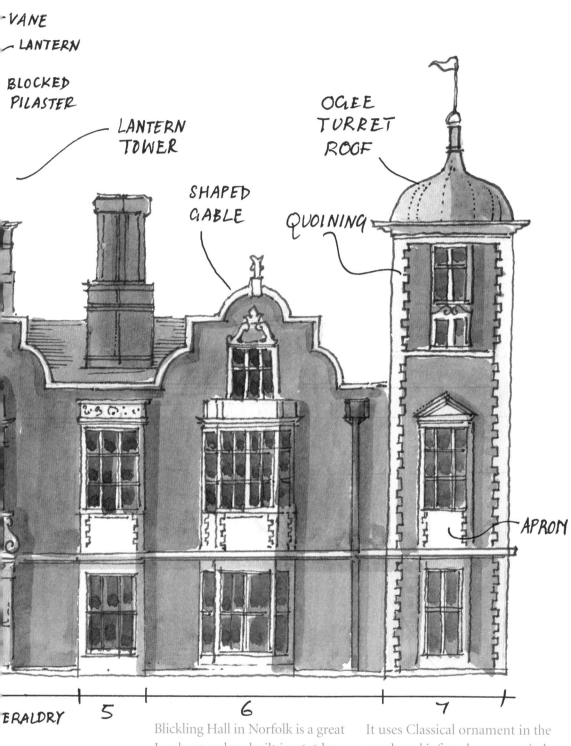

VANE

LANTERN

BLOCKED
PILASTER

LANTERN
TOWER

SHAPED
GABLE

OGEE
TURRET
ROOF

QUOINING

APRON

ERALDRY

5

6

7

Blickling Hall in Norfolk is a great
Jacobean palace built in 1616 by
the Lord Chief Justice. It was
designed by Robert Lyminge,
the architect of Hatfield House.

It uses Classical ornament in the
porch and is fiercely symmetrical.
The towers and delineated bays
foreshadow the coming Baroque
and Classical country houses.

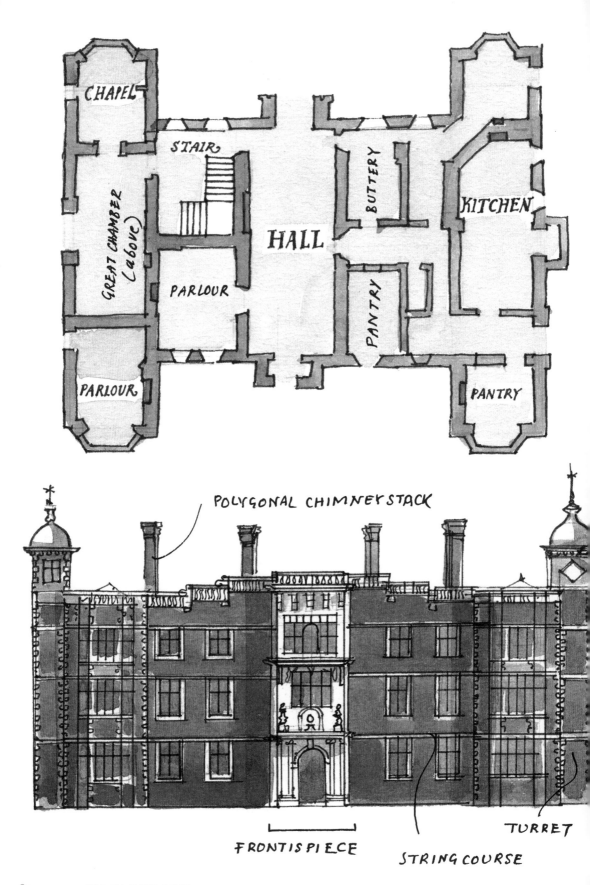

CHAPEL

STAIR

GREAT CHAMBER (above)

PARLOUR

PARLOUR

HALL

BUTTERY

PANTRY

KITCHEN

PANTRY

POLYGONAL CHIMNEY STACK

FRONTISPIECE

STRING COURSE

TURRET

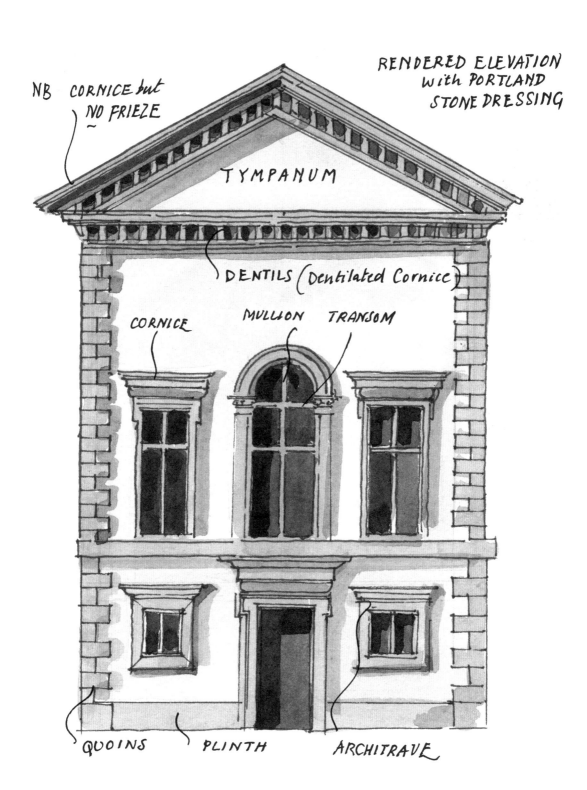

NB CORNICE but NO FRIEZE

RENDERED ELEVATION with PORTLAND STONE DRESSING

TYMPANUM

DENTILS (Dentilated Cornice)

CORNICE

MULLION   TRANSOM

QUOINS   PLINTH   ARCHITRAVE

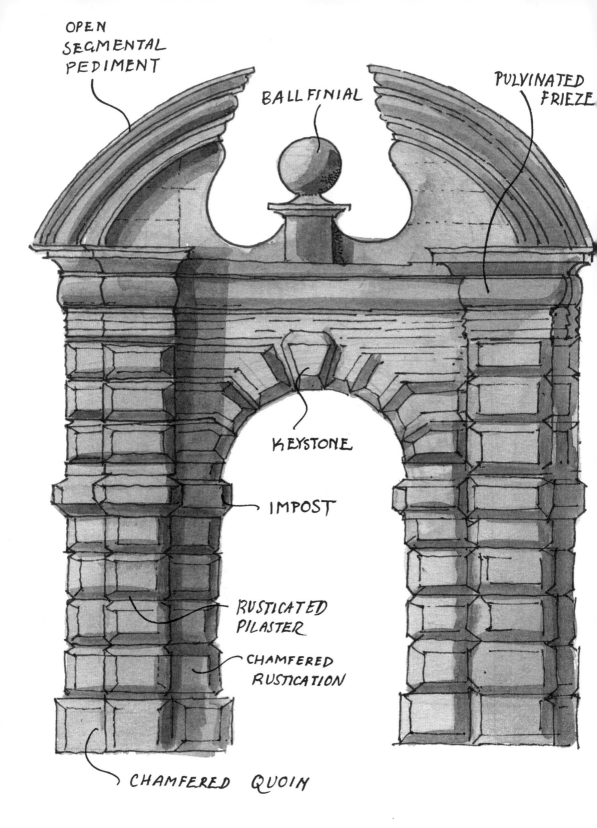

OPEN
SEGMENTAL
PEDIMENT

BALL FINIAL

PULVINATED
FRIEZE

KEYSTONE

IMPOST

RUSTICATED
PILASTER

CHAMFERED
RUSTICATION

CHAMFERED QUOIN

BUCRANIA   CORNICE

DORIC ENGAGED
COLUMNS

OBELISK

SWAN-NECKED PEDIMENT

PEDIMENT

HEAD STOP

ORIEL WINDOW

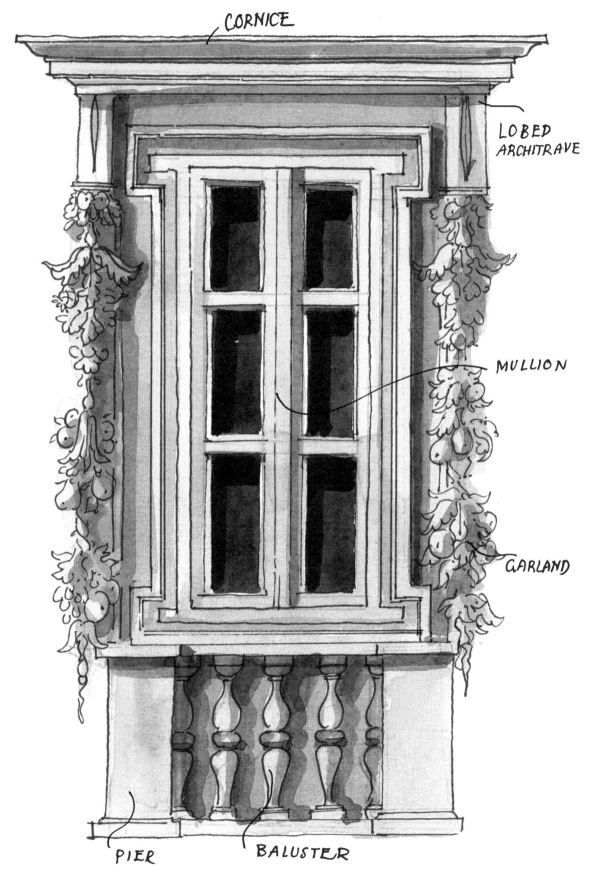

CORNICE

LOBED ARCHITRAVE

MULLION

GARLAND

PIER

BALUSTER

OPENWORK

GLORIA

QUOINS

DENTIL

RAIL

PIER

RENAISSANCE BALUSTER

COLONNETTES

SCROLL

OPENWORK

PEDIMENT

OBELISK

STRAPWORK

PARAPET

BLOCKED PILASTER

CAROLINE & QVEEN ANNE

The seventeenth century was turbulent and violent, and ended with revolution, albeit a relatively unbloody one. The Stuart kings were natural CATHOLICS, sympathisers if not actual practising Papists. They were, as a result, frequently at odds with their predominantly PROTESTANT subjects. The martyrdom of Charles I (1600–49) was the most dramatic instance of this, and the ensuing protectorate of Oliver Cromwell was, among other things, fiercely destructive to the architectural fabric of England's churches. The ICONOCLASTIC excesses of the ultra-Protestant Puritans wrought havoc on the fixtures and fittings of the parish church. Rood beams, screens and images, many of which had been restored to use during Archbishop Laud's primacy, were destroyed or lost. Statuary, carvings and paintings were smashed by zealots or hidden by pragmatic parishes. The Civil War also caused a cessation of major building projects among country-house owners, who were frequently subject to severe fines or confiscations.

Inigo Jones had introduced an austere CLASSICISM to England at the beginning of the century. His work was a complete departure from the muddled hotch-potch of applied Classical ornament that characterised the architecture of the late Elizabethan and Jacobean periods. With the accession of Charles I in 1625, the GRAND TOUR, the habit of well-born men taking off for an extended holiday to Europe, principally Italy, became established. As well as introducing young Englishmen to the charms of the BALMY SOUTH, it allowed them to visit for the first time the villas of ANDREA PALLADIO in the Veneto and to see his work and that of other RENAISSANCE and early BAROQUE architects in Florence, Rome and Venice. These compelling innovations were to have a dramatic effect on buildings at home and, by the 1640s, the old ways had yielded to a general acceptance of the 'uniforme and regular way of stone structure'. This meant the use of the Classical orders in a more or less literate way, adhering to the rules laid down in the works of Vitruvius, Serlio and Palladio. The PEDIMENT, the CORNICE and the GIANT ORDER, a pilaster that runs through more than one storey of a building, were now the features that dominated the elevations of new buildings.

The leading architects who interpreted this new style were Sir Roger Pratt (1620–85), John Webb (1611–72) and Hugh May (1621–84). However, many fine buildings were by lesser men, master masons, joiners and bricklayers. Their less-educated versions of the Classical model, often filtered through the more domestic style of the Dutch, is known as ARTISAN MANNERISM. Examples of such work, with imaginative but unacademic use of Classical components, often with sophisticated and technically skilful brickwork, can be seen both in London and in provincial towns. During the Commonwealth, there was building by the Parliamentary ascendancy, such as Thorpe Hall, designed by Peter Mills (c.1598–1670) in 1653, and now a Sue Ryder home in the unprepossessing outskirts of Peterborough. It is built in the Artisan mode, but in an orderly fashion, and has a splendid garden full of contemporary gateways, piers and doorways of real elegance.

SIR CHRISTOPHER WREN (1632–1723) did not start out as an architect. He was Savilian professor of astronomy at Oxford, a fellow of the Royal Society, an engineer and inventor. It was not until 1663 that he built his first building, the chapel at Pembroke College, Cambridge, where his uncle was Master. This was quickly followed by the Sheldonian Theatre in Oxford. These buildings follow the Roman example, but Wren had visited Paris in 1665, met Gianlorenzo Bernini (1598–1680) and Louis Le Vau (1612–70), and was influenced by their work at the Louvre and Vaux-le-Vicomte. Rather than using simple, solid masses, Wren articulated madly, projecting and withdrawing, stacking and curving, and inventing clever and sophisticated ways of treating an elevation. He was particularly occupied with the use of the DOME, which reached its apogee in the great double-skinned dome of St Paul's, begun in 1675 and completed in 1711.

In 1666, the GREAT FIRE OF LONDON consumed the greater part of the medieval city. This was an incredible opportunity to plan a new model capital, and Wren rose to the occasion. However, the radiating avenues of his new city were too daunting an innovation for the city fathers who, like Rotary Clubs the world over, were terrifyingly conservative, and a more modest reorganisation was embarked upon. The Act of Rebuilding of 1670 appointed commissioners Pratt, May and Wren to oversee the work, and some fifty NEW CHURCHES were proposed as a result. These are differing and exuberant variations on a theme, and most are still visible in the city today. Some are based on a simple Roman basilica plan using drawings from Vitruvius, and some draw from Italian Renaissance examples. Many had to contend with awkward sites inherited from their medieval predecessors. The grandest of all, St Stephen Walbrook (1672), was a forerunner of Wren's greatest work, St Paul's. Again, the architect found himself at odds with the conservative clients, the Corporation of London, but was so supported by his sovereign, that great PATRON OF THE ARTS Charles II (1630–85), that the final building was a genuinely new design.

His work in London meant that Wren was too busy to consider working outside the capital, which left the field clear for others, WILLIAM TALMAN (1650–1719), architect of Chatsworth with its dramatic giant orders; THOMAS ARCHER (1668–1743), who worked with Talman at Chatsworth and designed Heythrop; NICHOLAS HAWKSMOOR (1661–1736); and SIR JOHN VANBRUGH (1664–1726).

Hawksmoor assisted Wren at St Paul's, and produced six of London's finest BAROQUE churches himself, including St George's in Bloomsbury, St Mary Woolnoth in the City and Christ Church in Spitalfields. His work uses examples from Classical ANTIQUITY – the steeple of St George's, Bloomsbury, for example, draws on the Mausoleum of Halicarnassus for its singular form.

Vanbrugh, on the other hand, is best known for his country-house work. The great Baroque PALACES of Queen Anne's reign, on which he frequently worked with Hawksmoor, allowed the latter's knowledge of the work of Vitruvius and Serlio to complement the bravura genius of Vanbrugh. Thus was created the grandeur of Castle Howard, with colonnaded arms connecting the central block to pavilions, and the half-castle half-palace of Blenheim. Both appear to have more outside than in: Castle Howard has only one room, the Great Hall, that reflects the scale implied by the external elevation, and many of Blenheim's regiments of columns and gateways are, in fact, screens enclosing great courts, dramatising a visitor's arrival at this conquering hero's home.

Both these buildings, and the strangest of all, Seaton Delaval Hall in Northumberland, make use of RUSTICATION: breaking up the flat surface of an elevation into clearly delineated blocks of masonry, giving an impression of great muscularity and strength. Vanbrugh also uses ringed columns, whereby the same discipline is imposed on a column.

However, by the time of George I's accession to the throne, British patrons of architecture were ready for a change of diet.

BAY
WINDOW

QUOINS

STONE
DRESSINGS

SEGMENTAL
PEDIMENT

DUTCH GABLE
PEDIMENT

OPEN
SEGMENTAL
PEDIMENT

Swakeleys in Middlesex (1630) was built by Sir Robert Vyner, Lord Mayor of London. Pediments, plain and segmental, crown the windows, and elaborate Dutch gables top each bay, displaying the influence of Holland in the seventeenth century.

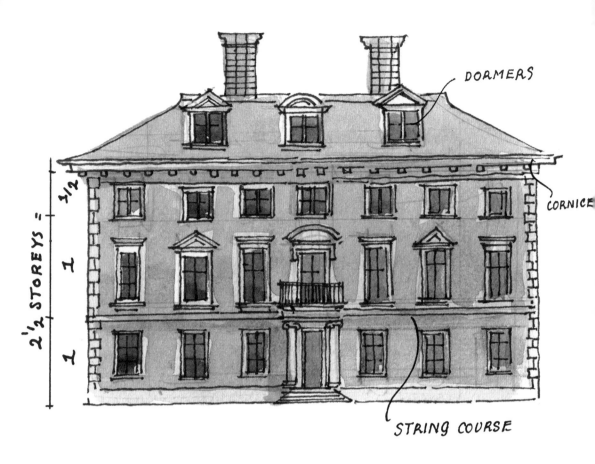

DORMERS

CORNICE

2½ STOREYS =

½

1

1

STRING COURSE

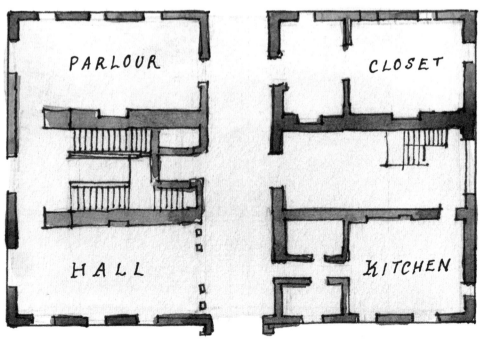

PARLOUR

CLOSET

HALL

KITCHEN

FESTOON PILASTER ESCUTCHEON

SEGMENTAL
PEDIMENT

SCROLLED
PEDIMENT

PLINTH

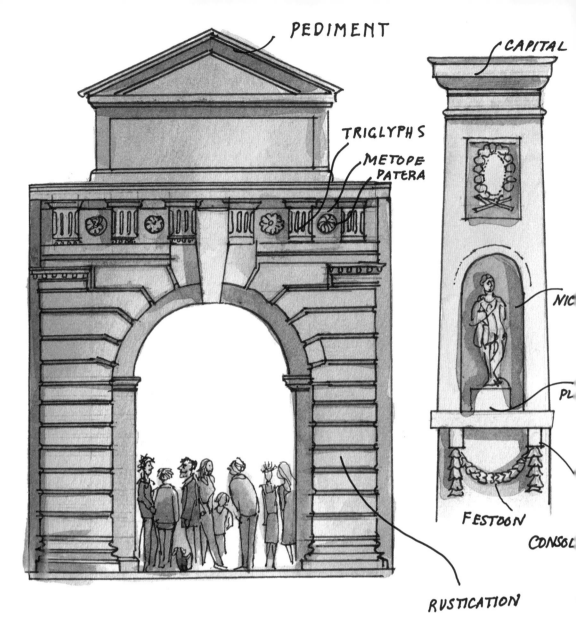

PEDIMENT

TRIGLYPHS

METOPE
PATERA

CAPITAL

NIC

PL

FESTOON

CONSOL

RUSTICATION

As the Baroque style developed, greater and greater liberties were taken with the elements of Classical architecture. For example, look at the archway above, with its exaggerated keystone, and the creation of an order with no shafts at all – just rustication.

SCROLL

PULVINATED FRIEZE

BANDED ARCHITRAVE

OPEN SEGMENTAL PEDIMENT

BROKEN PEDIMENT

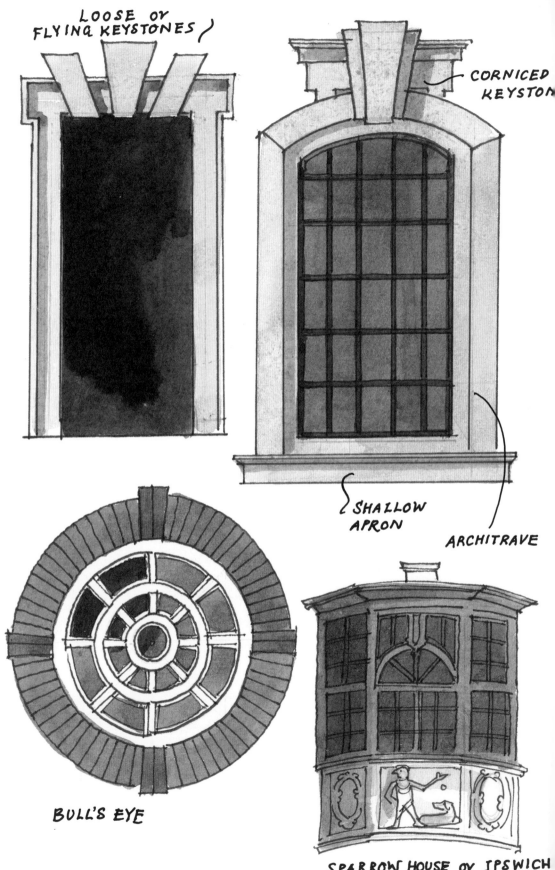

LOOSE or FLYING KEYSTONES

CORNICED KEYSTONE

SHALLOW APRON

ARCHITRAVE

BULL'S EYE

SPARROW HOUSE or IPSWICH WINDOW

BOW

SNAG or FESTOON

DECORATED KEYSTONE

SCROLLED PEDIMENT

PUTTO

SILL

APRON

SCROLL-TOPPED WINDOW

MULLION

CHIMNEY POT

CHIMNEY STACK

KEYSTONE

ROOFTOP ARCADE

CHIMNEY STACK DISGUISED as Battlement

OBELISK

FINIAL

STEPPED BATTLEMENTED PARAPET

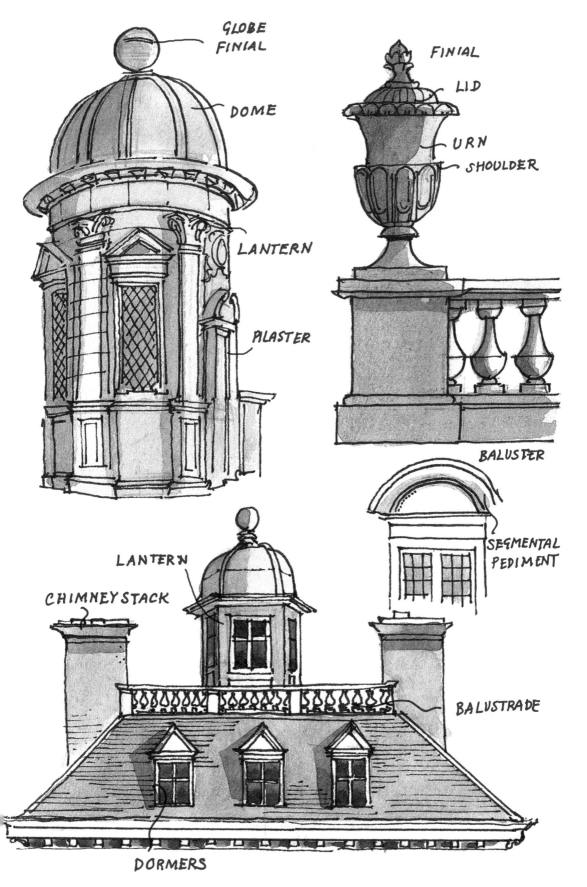

GLOBE FINIAL

DOME

LANTERN

PILASTER

FINIAL

LID

URN

SHOULDER

BALUSTER

SEGMENTAL PEDIMENT

LANTERN

CHIMNEY STACK

BALUSTRADE

DORMERS

GEORGIAN

The Baroque architects of the end of the seventeenth century and the very beginning of the eighteenth had strayed from the cool, Palladian order of Inigo Jones. When COLEN CAMPBELL (1676–1729) published his *Vitruvius Britannicus* in three volumes, number one in 1715, two in 1717, and three in 1725, he was not only illustrating the greatest country houses of the day, but also advertising his own work via his design for Wanstead. This great mansion was a return to the calculated austerity of Jones and Palladio, a building with 'no fancies or affectations'. The book was hugely influential, as was Giacomo Leoni's contemporary redrawing of Palladio's *Quattro Libri Dell'Architettura*. Leoni's publication contained engravings of all the great man's designs, built or unbuilt, in particular his series of VILLAS designed for the Venetian nobility in that city's mainland territories. The names of the Villas Barbero, Poiana, Malcontenta, Rotonda and Emo became well known in architectural circles, and their models closely copied. Consequently, there was a greater awareness of the direct source of Palladianism, and it became the style in which all new country houses were built.

Houghton Hall in Norfolk was among these, and one that would subsequently become influential in its own right. It was begun in 1722 by Campbell and completed after his death by JAMES GIBBS (1682–1754) in 1735. It drew heavily on the Jones design for Wilton of a century earlier, and had in common unfussy elevations. Nearby, at Holkham Hall, LORD BURLINGTON (1694–1753) and his protégé WILLIAM KENT (1685–1748), two more great names of the period, were at work for Thomas Coke, later Lord Leicester. He wanted a Palladian hall to house his collection of Classical sculpture acquired on a prolonged Grand Tour in Italy. Kent, originally a painter, had himself been in Italy from 1709 to 1719, during which time he met his patron, Burlington. Their design for Holkham Hall quotes directly from Palladio's Villa Mocenigo. This borrowing of designs was not a feeble cheat, but rather a definite effort to produce in England those buildings that were so desirable in Italy. Campbell's Mereworth Castle in Kent is a particularly attentive reproduction of Palladio's domed Villa Rotonda of 1566 outside Vicenza, sharing its elevations and plans.

The GROUND PLAN of these houses was of great importance: a succession of great, finely proportioned rooms leading from one to another, with their doors lined up so that a viewer might look through a long line of openings known as an ENFILADE. There are no corridors and none of the complexity of the Jacobean or earlier country houses; instead, these buildings are calm and orderly. Fireplaces and internal decorations are all in the same idiom, even if, as at Holkham Hall, the grandiose cornices and columns of the interior are in dramatic contrast to the austere plainness of the façade. Much used were VENETIAN, or SERLIAN, windows: tripartite panes under a common surround in which the central section is raised and arched.

The whole idea for Lord Burlington's own Chiswick House (1725) beside the Thames was derived from the work of Palladio, and through him from the Romans. It was a domestic retreat away from the city in an idyllic setting. Still a high-status building, the villa was the opposite of a castle, being neither defensive nor martial. In their original Roman form, villas were intended as a place for learned pursuits, as well as a site for the improvement of agriculture, a subject dear to the Roman gentleman's heart. This ideal became immediately popular in Britain, although the temple front was extended by WINGS, SCREENS and PAVILIONS to fulfil the vast requirements of size, as at Holkham.

The mid-eighteenth century also saw major developments in TOWN PLANNING. In newly fashionable Bath, JOHN WOOD (1704–54) and his son, also John (1728–81), built elegant streets inspired by Roman ideas of grandeur that included the splendid Circus and Ionic Royal Crescent. Through *An Essay towards a Description of Bath* (1742, revised 1749), their ideas proved hugely influential, particularly in Edinburgh's New Town and in John Nash's plans for London.

ROBERT ADAM (1728–92) was the son of the Scottish architect William Adam (1689–1748). As did many noted NEO-CLASSICISTS, he completed his education in Italy, but a little later (1754–7). Like them, he studied the ruins of ancient Rome, and published a set of drawings of DIOCLETIAN'S palace in Split. He was also inspired by the elaborate architectural *capriccios* of PIRANESI. These engravings of soaring, crumbling, ruined buildings, ancient prisons and palaces overgrown with ivy were to have as great an influence on his work as they did on his contemporary William Chambers (1722–96), the designer of Somerset House in London, who was in Italy in 1750. These eighteenth-century architects studied the antique not through pattern books as their predecessors did, or through the lens of the French or Dutch, but directly from THE ANCIENTS. Each one of them brought back to England new examples and a new understanding of the use of the CLASSICAL ORDERS.

Indeed, Adam made use of actual antiquities in his own buildings, not in the way that Kent had decorated Holkham's rooms with Coke's Classical sculpture, but by actually reusing ancient columns dredged from the River Tiber as structural components in the anteroom to the great hall at Syon House in west London. Adam's researches had given him evidence of the use of COLOUR in Classicism, and his interiors are rich and elaborate, a striking development from the cool calm of his predecessors. His elegant interior decoration was also inspired by the antique, and his delicate, shallow-vaulted ceilings and apses used decorations from the newly discovered wall paintings in the ruins of POMPEII, excavations of which had begun in 1748.

In 1760, Adam took over the building of Kedleston Hall in Derbyshire from Matthew Brettingham (1699–1769). As well as the Classical house, which comprised a central temple front connected by wings to two pavilions, the format established by Campbell at Wanstead (see page 102), Adam built a fishing hut in the 'GOTHICK' taste. This was a stone box with Gothic tracery in the windows, pinnacles and shafts, an advance view of the early nineteenth-century Gothic Revival known as 'STRAWBERRY HILL GOTHICK'. Horace Walpole (son of Robert, who built Houghton) built his villa, Strawberry Hill in Twickenham, from 1750. His decorative but unscholarly use of Gothic elements is airy and elegant, but the Gothic has not been digested. It is merely used as an applied style. This 'Gothick' taste is not only a manifestation of ANTIQUARIANISM in architecture, but a political statement, as the Gothic was a style of Tory opposition. Much play was made of the idea of the Gothic, oddly also referred to as Saxon, representing the nation's ancient liberties being eroded by the Whig government. However, in fact, the Gothic style had never completely disappeared. Throughout the late sixteenth and early seventeenth centuries, the Gothic survived where it was considered appropriate, such as in OXFORD or CAMBRIDGE COLLEGES, an environment where being 'in keeping' was desirable.

This was not a great period for CHURCH building. The 1711 Act for fifty new churches (see page 90) that gave rise to so many of the capital's great buildings was the last such action until the Church Building Act of 1818, which filled the newly constructed city suburbs with non-Conformist rabble-quelling establishments of unexciting design. With the ENLIGHTENMENT, the great extension of intellectual advance in science and engineering and the arts that coloured the eighteenth century, the Church was rather in the background. Although England continued to attend the services of the Church of England, the parish church was not the focus of architectural attention that it had been at the turn of the century, and, in rural parishes, churches frequently fell into disrepair or even disuse.

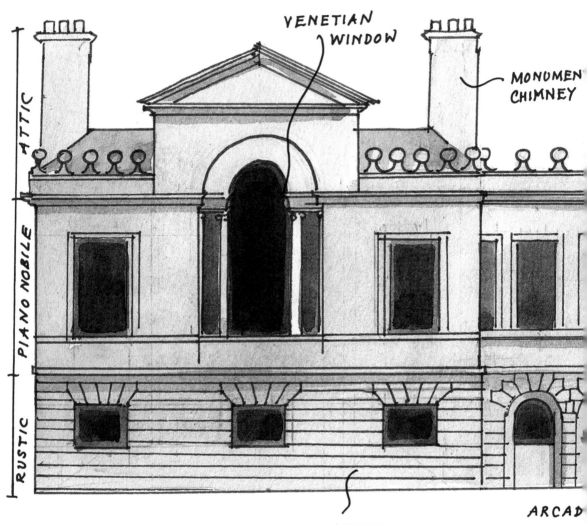

VENETIAN WINDOW

MONUMEN CHIMNEY

ATTIC

PIANO NOBILE

RUSTIC

RUSTICATED GROUND FLOOR

ARCAD

This is New Wardour Castle, built for the Arundel family by James Paine in 1769. It is as quintessentially Georgian as they come – cool and austere with pediments and a rusticated ground floor. The three-bay pavilions at either end are connected to the central block by arcades.

BLOCKING
COURSE

STRING COURSE

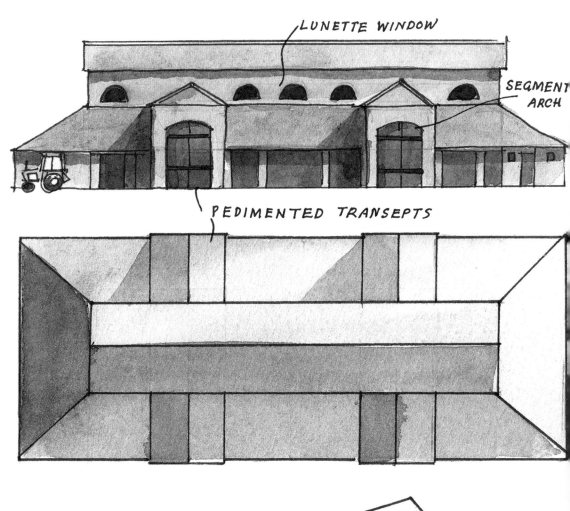

LUNETTE WINDOW

SEGMENT ARCH

PEDIMENTED TRANSEPTS

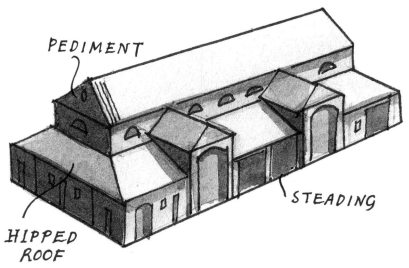

PEDIMENT

STEADING

HIPPED ROOF

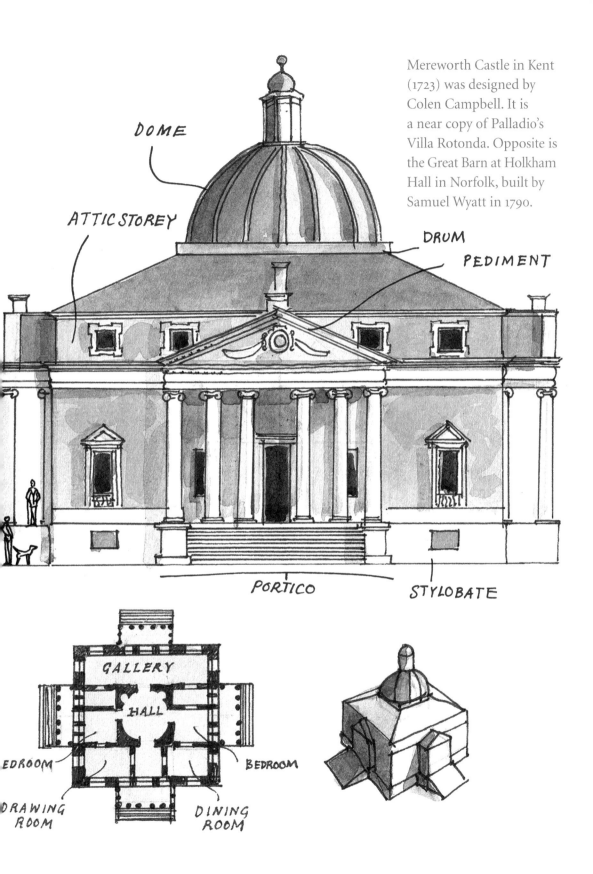

DOME

ATTIC STOREY

DRUM

PEDIMENT

PORTICO

STYLOBATE

GALLERY

HALL

EDROOM

BEDROOM

DRAWING
ROOM

DINING
ROOM

Mereworth Castle in Kent (1723) was designed by Colen Campbell. It is a near copy of Palladio's Villa Rotonda. Opposite is the Great Barn at Holkham Hall in Norfolk, built by Samuel Wyatt in 1790.

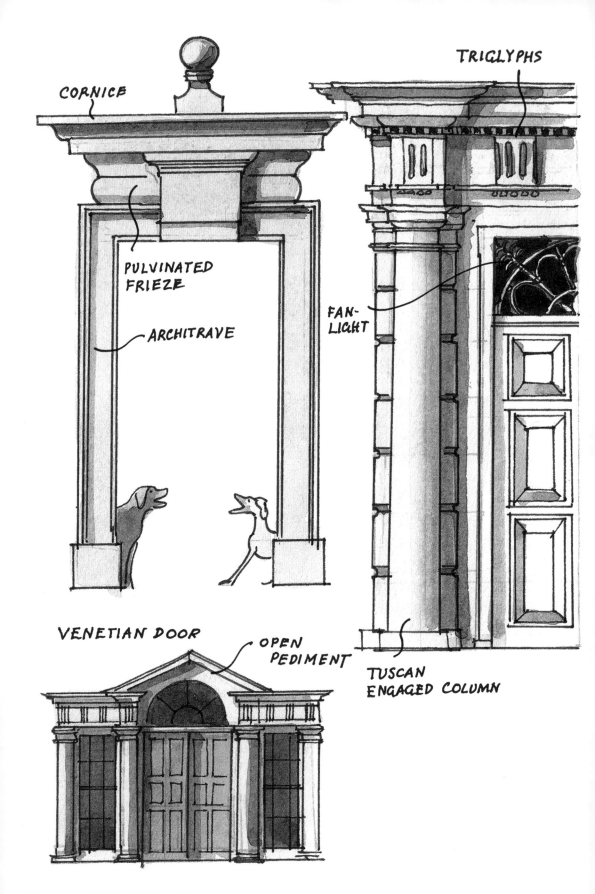

CORNICE

TRIGLYPHS

PULVINATED
FRIEZE

ARCHITRAVE

FAN-
LIGHT

VENETIAN DOOR

OPEN
PEDIMENT

TUSCAN
ENGAGED COLUMN

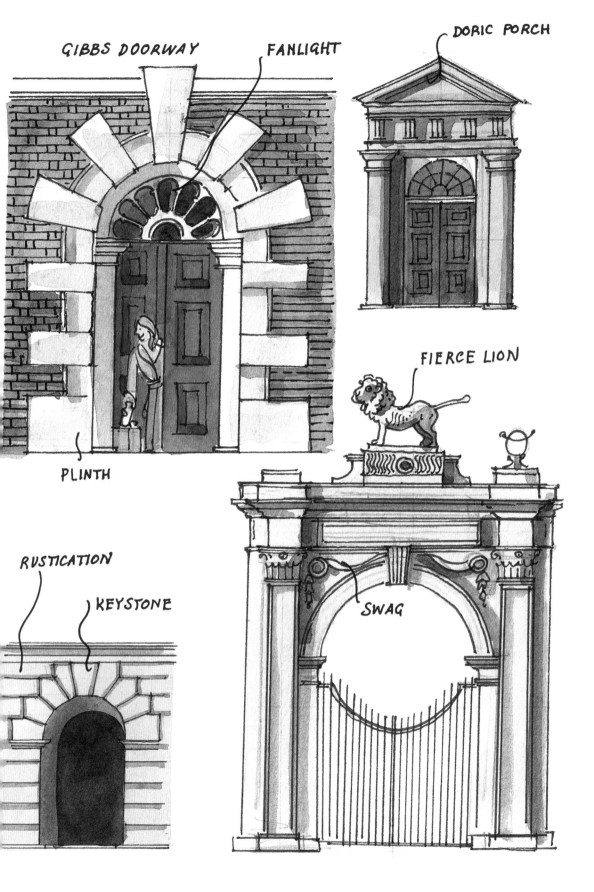

GIBBS DOORWAY

FANLIGHT

DORIC PORCH

PLINTH

FIERCE LION

RUSTICATION

KEYSTONE

SWAG

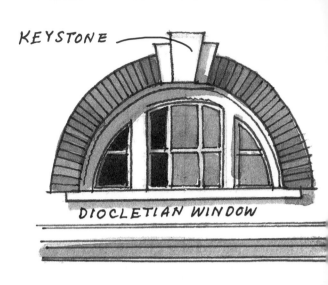

KEYSTONE

DIOCLETIAN WINDOW

The sash window reigned throughout this period; however, it came wearing much fancy dress, with Chinese, 'Gothick' or Classical variations of differing complexity.

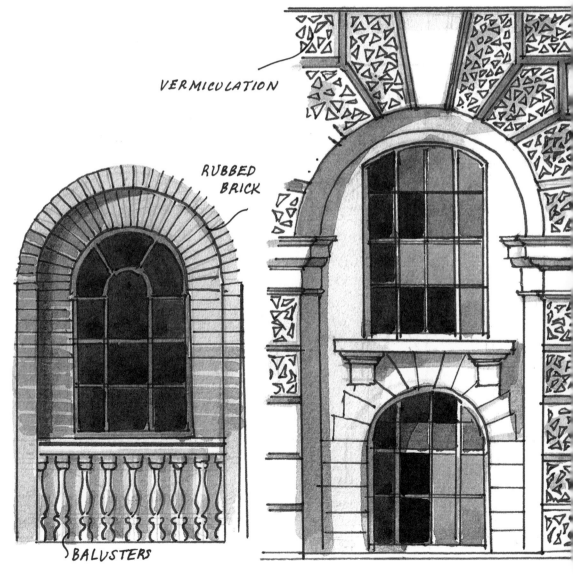

VERMICULATION

RUBBED BRICK

BALUSTERS

OGEE

STRAWBERRY HILL GOTHICK

CHINESE CHIPPENDALE TYPE GLAZING

EACH DIVISION IS A LIGHT i.e. this is a TWELVE-LIGHT WINDOW

VENETIAN WINDOW

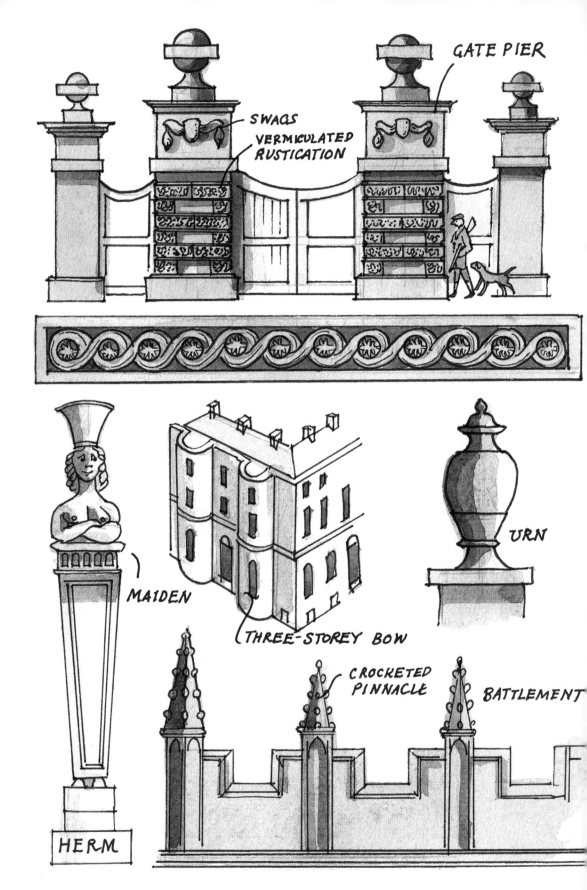

GATE PIER

SWAGS

VERMICULATED RUSTICATION

MAIDEN

THREE-STOREY BOW

URN

HERM

CROCKETED PINNACLE

BATTLEMENT

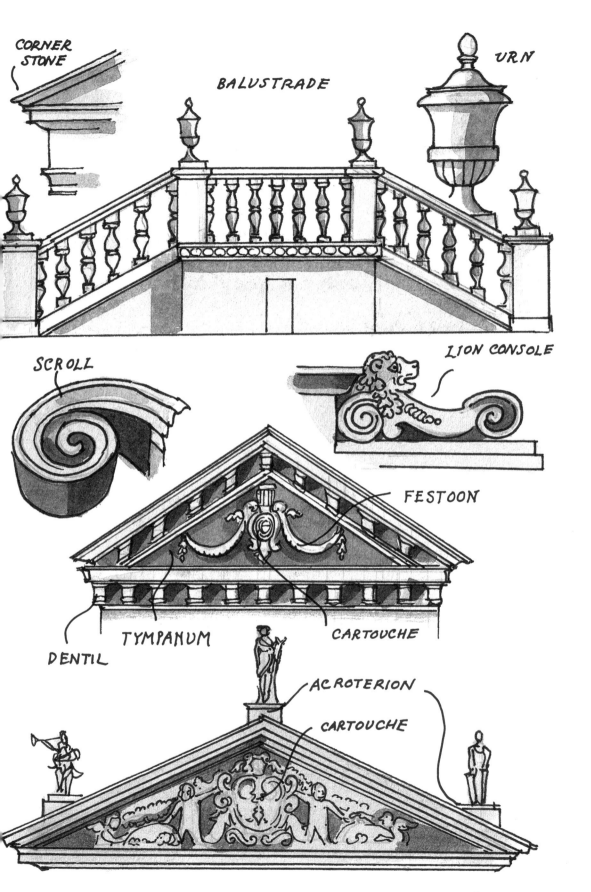

CORNER STONE

BALUSTRADE

URN

SCROLL

LION CONSOLE

FESTOON

TYMPANUM

CARTOUCHE

DENTIL

ACROTERION

CARTOUCHE

REGENCY

The actual REGENCY, the period during which the wild, sensual and dissolute Prince of Wales assumed power while his father, George III, was insane lasted from 1811 to 1820. However, in architectural terms, it covers the last years of the eighteenth century and continues throughout George IV's actual reign and that of his jolly brother William IV until the accession of Victoria in 1837.

Architecturally, it sees the introduction of the PICTURESQUE and instigates the REVIVALISM and ECLECTICISM of the nineteenth century. The early period is dominated by JAMES WYATT (1746–1813), the showy rival of Robert Adam whose *tour de force* and nemesis was the extraordinary confection of Fonthill Abbey, built between 1795 and 1807. This defining Romantic pile was cruciform in plan and soared to the heavens with an octagonal lantern visible for miles. Unfortunately it was structurally unsound and, twenty years later, tumbled to the ground with a force that blew the butler from one end of a passage to the other. It was, however, decidedly Picturesque.

The desire for a romantic vision was inspired in part by the writing of RICHARD PAYNE KNIGHT (1750–1824). He was a full-lipped and bushy-whiskered classical scholar and connoisseur whose wish was to see the beauties of painting, in particular those of the seventeenth-century landscape painter Claude Lorrain, translated into actual landscapes and buildings. This provided the intellectual background for JOHN NASH (1752–1835), who built just such irregularly profiled villas of an imagined Italian *campagna*, and Nash's sometime business partner HUMPHRY REPTON (1752–1818), the greatest landscape architect of the age. Repton had assumed the mantle of LANCELOT 'CAPABILITY' BROWN (1716–83), the driving force in the move to sweep away the radiating avenues and formal parterres that surround the houses shown in *Vitruvius Britannicus* and replace them with artfully scattered clumps of trees. Repton, inspired by the writing of Payne Knight and Payne Knight's Herefordshire neighbour Uvedale Price, sought to further informalise landscapes and, where creating new ones, to retain, as far as possible, all gnarled old oaks and other features of a Picturesque nature. To set out his schemes to improve a landscape and its mansion, Repton would produce a RED BOOK. These sketchbooks, with their beautiful watercolour renderings, used flaps and folds to reveal a before and after view of the park in question. Many still survive, often in the houses they illustrated.

Nash also designed many Picturesque LODGES, DAIRIES and COTTAGES. Some are proto-Classical in an imagined style of the ancient Greek countryside, branched logs complete with bark taking the place of columns with simplified pediments of wood above. Others are ITALIANATE and still others are GOTHIC, or even thatched in a formalised neo-vernacular that predates the vernacular revival cottages of Ernest Gimson by a century. Nash's best-known examples are in the model village at Blaise Hamlet, Gloucestershire (1810). Here perfect *Hansel and Gretel* cottages cluster, without rudely jostling, around a little village green. The houses, for they are of a more commodious size than any real cottage, have features not usually associated with the lives of horny-handed sons of the soil – such as loggias and wrap-around wooden benches that would accommodate whole villages of paupers. Yet they were built for the retired farmworkers of the Quaker

John Scandrett Harford (1787–1866) in a style he obviously felt appropriate. His own house, Blaise Castle, is an unexceptional late eighteenth-century Classical block with no hint of the Picturesque.

Nash was not limited to Romantic country houses and their dependencies, and by 1798 he was designing for the Prince of Wales. His partnership with Repton was cast aside as he moved on to greater things, and in 1811–12 he embarked on the grandiose plans for Regent's Park and a great thoroughfare, Regent Street, to connect it with St James's. Here villas of the Italianate persuasion and great curving CIRCUSES and TERRACES of stuccoed town houses were grouped together in a startlingly new way. In the park itself the villas were shrouded in trees in a Romantic landscape, the centrepiece of which was to have been a royal residence, but was never built. In the terraces and streets to the south, pedimented, domed and be-pillared façades joined together to form elaborate and well-articulated views. This was the first and last time any serious planning had gone on in London in the way carried out by Baron Haussmann in Paris later in the nineteenth century. Nash's genius was for planning and overview, rather than for detailing, which is often coarse and heavy in his work.

Other styles were making themselves felt. The Gothic that surfaced for breath in the mid-eighteenth century at Strawberry Hill was taken further by Jeffry Wyatt when he was working at Windsor Castle in the 1820s. His Orangery there uses a Classicised late Perpendicular in an efficient, but slightly charmless way. The REGENCY GOTHIC has neither Strawberry Hill's filigree frou-frou charm nor any indication of the earnest Gothic that Pugin was waiting to unleash.

A fashion for the INDIAN taste grew out of England's gradual domination of that subcontinent, as returning *nabobs* recreated the comforts of their recent tropical past. This saw the introduction of the VERANDA to British architecture, which reached its apogee in Nash's fantasy at the Brighton Pavilion and S. P. Cockerell's Sezincote (1803).

Much more significant than this nascent orientalism was the GREEK REVIVAL. In the mid-eighteenth century, James 'Athenian'

Stuart (1713–88) visited Greece and saw that Rome was not the only pure source of Classicism, indeed, that it was itself derived from the GREEK model. Fifty years later, William Wilkins (1778–1839) produced designs for Downing College in Cambridge in which a Greek Ionic order, that of the Erechtheum in Athens, was employed. This new CLASSICISM did away with pilasters and decorative fripperies and was a conscious return to a primitive and muscular form. In 1806, Wilkins built Grange Park near Alresford in Hampshire. This is now a controlled ruin, but summer visitors to the opera held inside the shell of the old ballroom can still walk through the massive Doric portico. Ironically, in its ruined state, it combines the two opposing schools of early nineteenth-century architectural thought, as its muscular, pure Grecianism is overlaid with ruinous Romanticism.

The last of the Regency giants is SIR JOHN SOANE (1753–1837), although he worked in the late Georgian period as well. Soane travelled to Italy in 1778–80 under the patronage of George III, and there developed an idiosyncratic version of the Palladian ideal. In 1788, he became architect of the Bank of England and designed several rooms for it, all now demolished. They made tremendous use of a shallow SEGMENTAL ARCH and similarly shaped shallow DOMES and CROSS-VAULTED CEILINGS. These features are visible today in his own house in Lincoln's Inn Fields, now the Sir John Soane's Museum, and at the extraordinary and Vanbrugh-like Dulwich Picture Gallery, but they can be more commonly seen, albeit in a slightly debased form, in the roof of the red telephone box.

The massive Greek neo-Classicism of the National Gallery, University College and the British Museum were, for the time being, the end of Classicism. Cockerell's Ashmolean Museum (1845) in Oxford is its wild last gasp, but builders were seeking a new style. Both Sir Charles Barry (1795–1860) at the Manchester Art Gallery (1824) and the Travellers Club (1829), and Decimus Burton (1800–81) at the Athenaeum (1827) looked to the Italian Renaissance for inspiration, and offer a foretaste of the frantic dash around the styles of architectural revivals that characterises the rest of the nineteenth century.

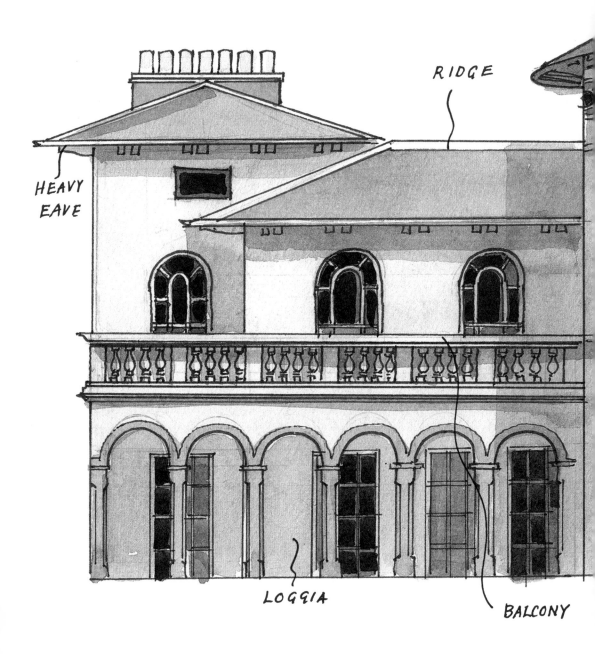

RIDGE

HEAVY
EAVE

LOGGIA

BALCONY

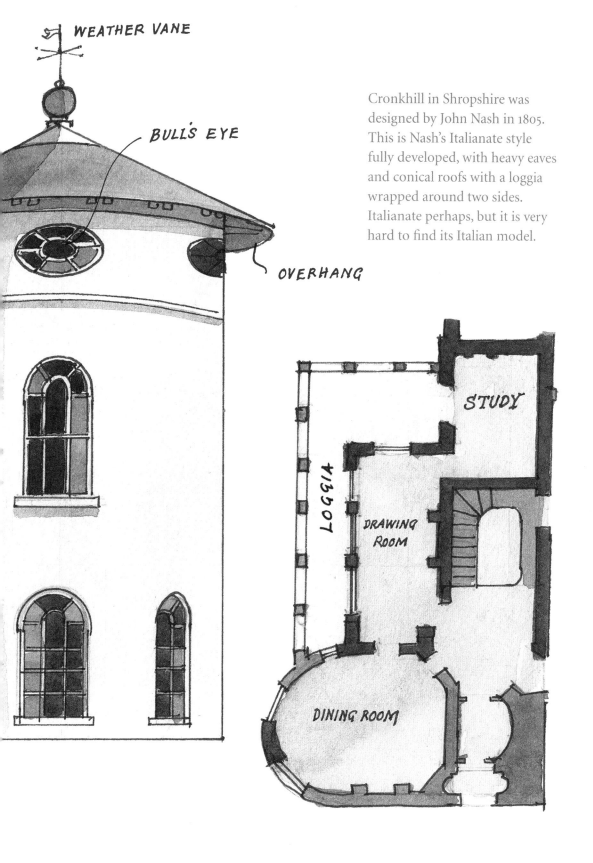

WEATHER VANE

BULL'S EYE

OVERHANG

Cronkhill in Shropshire was designed by John Nash in 1805. This is Nash's Italianate style fully developed, with heavy eaves and conical roofs with a loggia wrapped around two sides. Italianate perhaps, but it is very hard to find its Italian model.

STUDY

LOGGIA

DRAWING ROOM

DINING ROOM

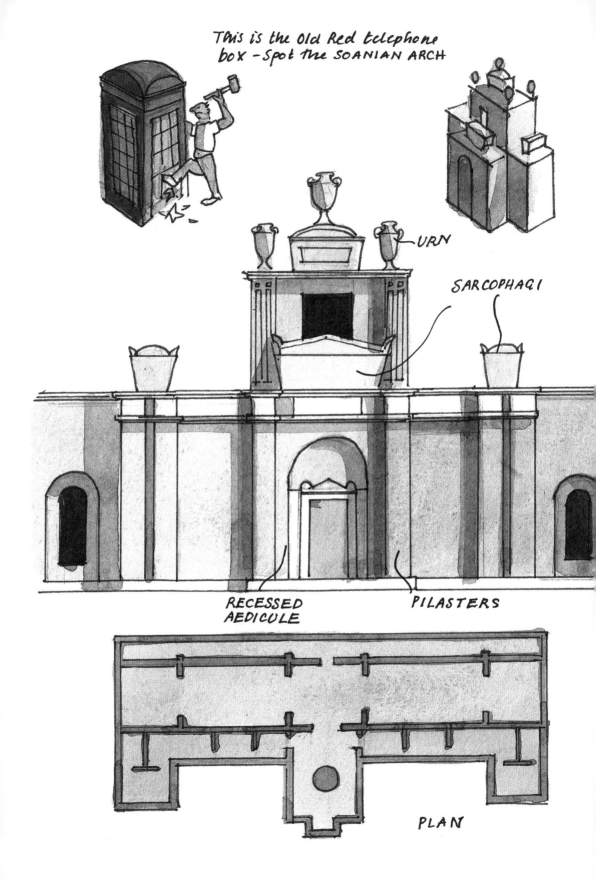

This is the Old Red telephone box - Spot the SOANIAN ARCH

URN

SARCOPHAGI

RECESSED
AEDICULE

PILASTERS

PLAN

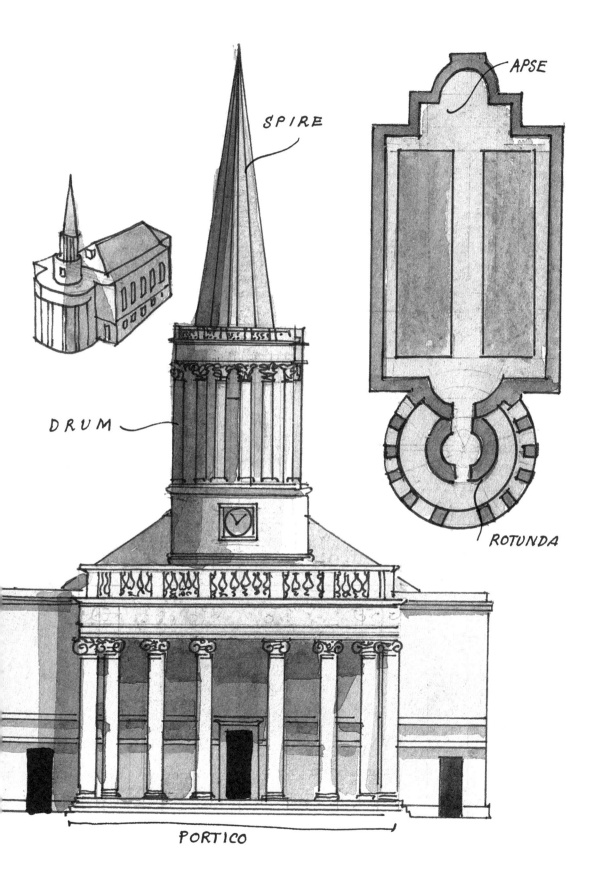

SPIRE

APSE

DRUM

ROTUNDA

PORTICO

HOOD MOULD

INDO-GOTHIC ARCH

PICTURESQUE PORCH

GOTHIC FINIAL

ORIENTAL PORCH

LANTE

CAST-IRON
FANLIGHT

CAST-IRON PORCH

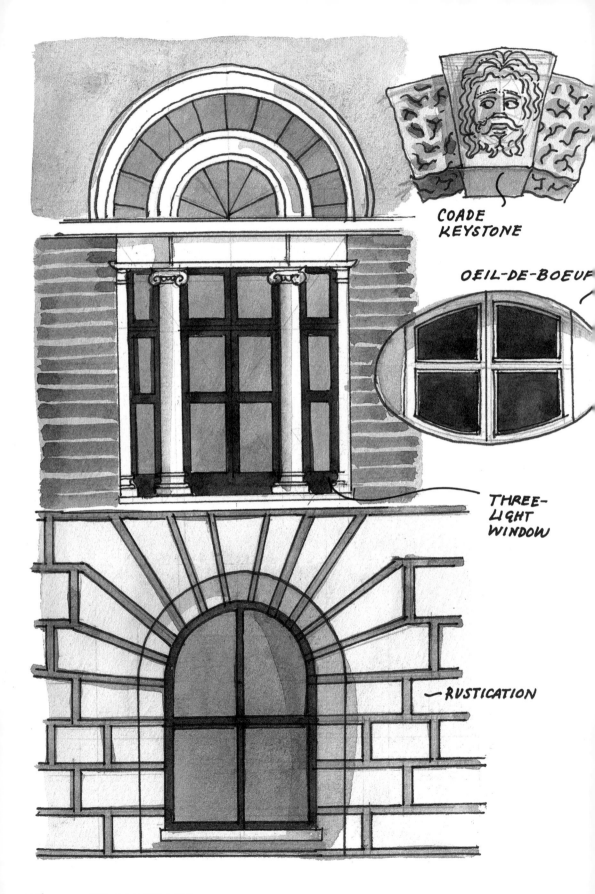

COADE
KEYSTONE

OEIL-DE-BOEUF

THREE-
LIGHT
WINDOW

—RUSTICATION

GOTHIC ARCH

EARLY C19 PERPENDICULAR-STYLE GOTHIC TRACERY

DEPRESSED ARCH

LUNETTE WINDOW

BULL'S EYE

OGIVAL CUSPING

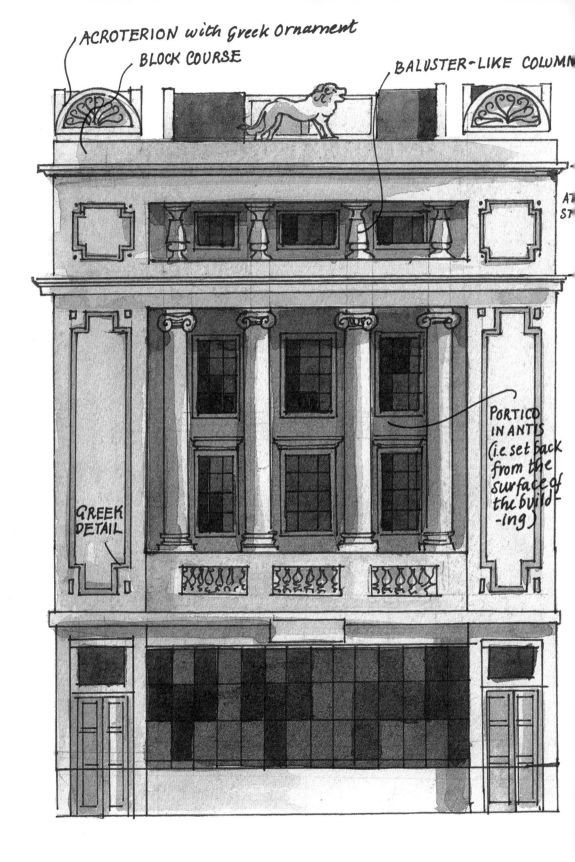

ACROTERION with Greek Ornament

BLOCK COURSE

BALUSTER-LIKE COLUMN

ATTIC STOREY

PORTICO IN ANTIS (i.e. set back from the surface of the building)

GREEK DETAIL

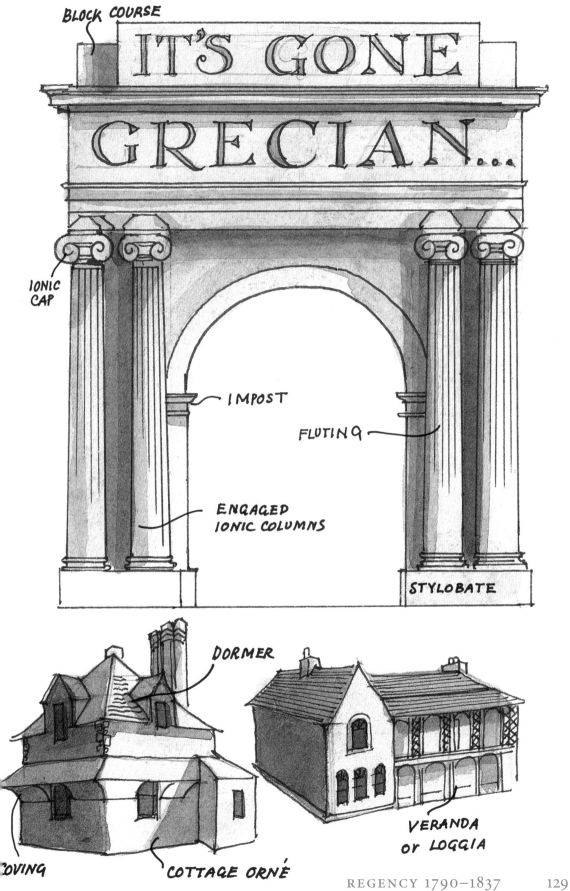

BLOCK COURSE

IT'S GONE

GRECIAN....

IONIC CAP

IMPOST

FLUTING

ENGAGED IONIC COLUMNS

STYLOBATE

DORMER

'OVING

COTTAGE ORNÉ

VERANDA or LOGGIA

EARLY VICTORIAN

After the louche excesses of the sons of George III, the accession of a pretty and virtuous girl of eighteen to the throne marked a change in British society, typified by the Municipal Reform Act of 1835. This Act, fiercely contended with great vigour by the aristocratic forces of reaction, sought to end the rotten boroughs and to move slowly towards what was then seen as UNIVERSAL SUFFRAGE. The boroughs were archaic parliamentary constituencies often physically non-existent, the votes of which were controlled by landed magnates, who could easily block liberal legislation. The new system was far from the one-person one-vote way of today, but it at least allowed every freeholding male to have an equal say. This in itself was seen by many as seditious folly in an age when rolling revolution and drastic change was raging through mainland Europe.

Greater freedoms – the Roman Catholics were emancipated in 1829 – and the continuing and unstoppable advance of the Industrial Revolution represented seismic changes to society. As more and more of the valleys of the north-west filled with cotton mills and factories, a reaction set in. Most extreme, but still representative of these views, were those of AUGUSTUS W. N. PUGIN (1812–52).

Of all the GOTHIC REVIVALISTS who swept away the last vestiges of Classicism in the early nineteenth century, it was Pugin who was most influential. His father was a French émigré, one of many who migrated to England during the turbulent years at the end of the eighteenth century. Father and son worked together as architectural draughtsmen, realising the designs of Nash and Repton. The younger Pugin soon developed a dislike for the superficial use of the Gothic as merely a dressing for otherwise Classical buildings. He was a great ANTIQUARIAN, collecting manuscripts, sculpture and stained-glass fragments on his trips around northern Europe. He sketched domestic and ecclesiastical medieval buildings, studying their construction and the grammar of their elaborate tracery.

Pugin's career was short; he died, exhausted, at forty, but designed dozens of churches and cathedrals, and collaborated on many others. Most notable of these was Charles Barry's new HOUSES OF PARLIAMENT, where all the lavish interiors and the greater part of the exterior detail was by Pugin's hand. His pattern books of Gothic decoration were hugely influential on his many imitators, and by his death in 1852 his POINTED STYLE and developments in the NEO-GOTHIC held sway throughout Britain and its growing empire. Most typical of his remaining work, the greater part of which was obliterated during the twentieth century, is St Giles' church in Cheadle, Staffordshire (1846). It is a romp in the revived DECORATED style, with polychrome decoration, encaustic tiles made by Minton in nearby Stoke-on-Trent, elaborate metalwork and stencilled painting. Significant is the inclusion of a rood screen, a component of the church interior that had all but disappeared at the Reformation.

By the end of the eighteenth century, the Church of England had atrophied into a series of sinecures supporting idle and often absent pluralist priests. These were clerics who benefited from the income of two or more parishes, with an impecunious curate to carry out their pastoral duties. The reign of Victoria saw a dramatic change, with the rise of HIGH CHURCH ANGLICANISM, Tractarians, the Oxford Movement and the Cambridge Camden society on one side, and the zeal of EVANGELICAL CHRISTIANITY on the other. The High Church side saw a dissolute and enfeebled

Church, and felt that a return to pre-Reformation ways was desirable. This meant a more mysterious and liturgically complex kind of worship in which the Eucharist, not the sermon, should be the centre of a service, as had been the case in the Protestant Church since the sixteenth century. This change of emphasis was reflected in new churches, where the ALTAR rather than the PULPIT became the architectural focus.

These two movements, and their rejuvenating effects on the established Church, led to a great rebuilding of churches, both muscular EARLY GOTHIC REVIVAL and later HIGH VICTORIAN. The Roman Catholic Church was also invigorated. Pugin, who converted to Rome himself, was responsible for several of the first Catholic churches to be built since the Reformation, such as the Roman Catholic cathedrals of Nottingham and Birmingham.

Pugin was not alone. He was at the forefront of the Gothic Revivalists, but Charles Barry, George Edmund Street, George Gilbert Scott and, later, William Burges and William Butterfield all worked in and developed the Gothic style. From 1845 until the 1870s the fashion drifted through EARLY ENGLISH, DECORATED and ROMANESQUE, the last also known by its delicious German name, *Rundbogenstil*. The intention to display the construction of a building was now the driving force, and all decoration was to emphasise that construction. Thus a staircase, which had for two and a half centuries been an internal feature of a house and unseen from the outside, might now be marked by ascending narrow Gothic windows that traced its progress up the building. A kitchen might have its great chimney emphasised rather than concealed within the once-vital symmetry of the elevation. Examples of English Gothic architecture took on the significance of Classicism's Palladian exemplars: instead of the Villa Rotonda, the Abbot's Kitchen at Glastonbury was to have far-reaching influence through its nineteenth-century progeny, such as the Museum of Natural History at Oxford.

The first part of Victoria's reign was not all incense, prayer and austere medievalism. It also saw the continuation of the world's first

INDUSTRIAL REVOLUTION. More and more factories were thrown up in the industrial north, and although some survive, such as those by Titus Salt at Saltaire of 1853, many have disappeared with their industries. Visitors to Stoke-on-Trent, home of Staffordshire's once world-dominating ceramics industry, will drive through hundreds of acres of pummelled brickdust prairie, looking in vain for the factories that produced Mason's Ironstone, New Hall porcelain or Doulton. The skyline of blackened brick bottle kilns and chimneys has gone. Only the odd tombstone tooth remains in the wasteland.

The most powerful single symbol of newly developed Britain was the RAILWAY. From 1837, when the London & Birmingham Railway built its first terminus at Euston Square, the railway station and its attendant hotel became a dominant building type. Euston was first, with a Doric portico and flanking lodges designed by Philip Hardwick (1792–1870). This style was familiar from the gates of large country houses, but over the next ten years a monumental Italianate style developed at London Bridge, Nine Elms and Bricklayer's Arms stations. In 1851, the Great Northern Railway began to build King's Cross, a magnificent symbol of the New Age. A suitably grand engineering problem was presented by the sheds themselves, as they required roofs of a huge span. Those at King's Cross were 105ft wide, and the widest, at Paddington, designed by that giant of nineteenth-century engineering ISAMBARD KINGDOM BRUNEL (1806–59), was 110ft wide.

Those of a modernistic bent are inclined to look at these feats of engineering as the Victorians' greatest architectural legacy, admiring the bold and innovative technologies employed. However, what makes the experience of alighting in these buildings so thrilling is not only the simple curve of the roof or even the many platforms; it is the generous combination of engineering with GOTHIC DECORATION. Tracery, mouchettes, daggers and all manner of cusping decorate the steel beams and the end walls of the sheds. Under these, the locomotives steaming off to Oxford, Swansea or Penzance are not an austere semi-circle of functionality, but rather a sinuous pattern of swirling steel adding dignity to the design. It was, after all, VICTORIAN.

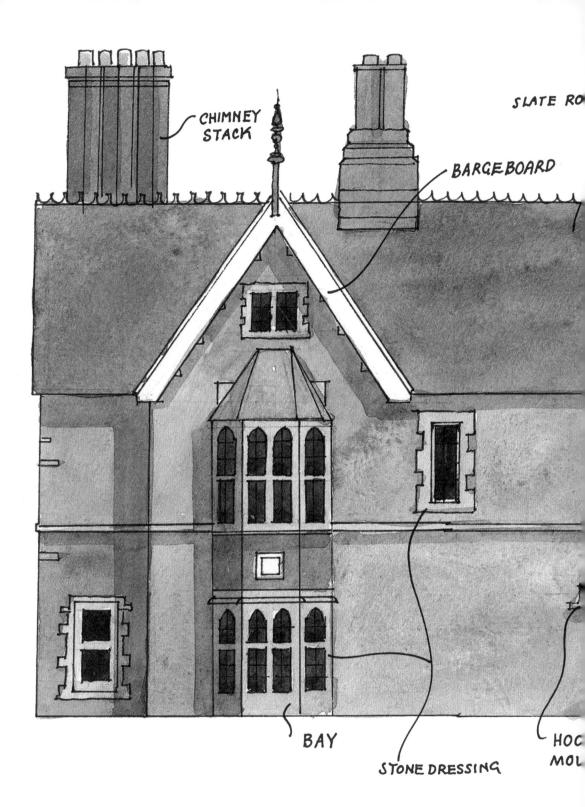

CHIMNEY STACK

SLATE RO[OF]

BARGEBOARD

BAY

STONE DRESSING

HOO[D]
MOL[D]

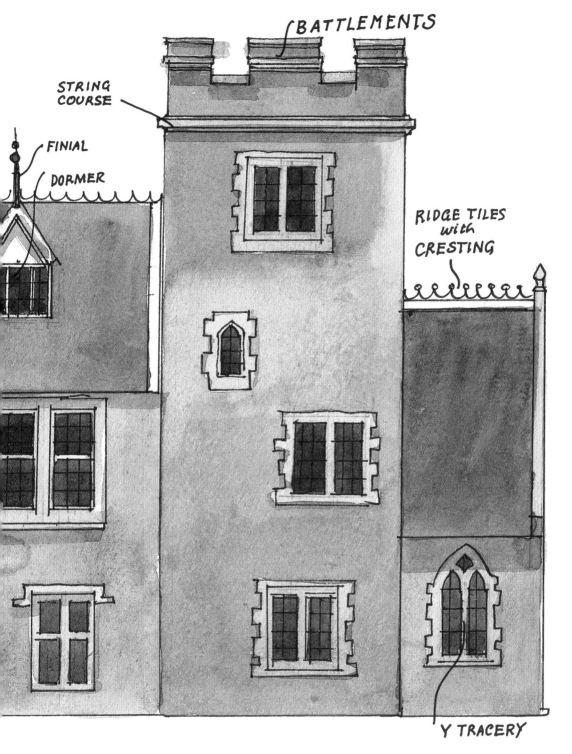

BATTLEMENTS

STRING COURSE

FINIAL

DORMER

RIDGE TILES with CRESTING

Y TRACERY

St Augustine's Grange was built by Pugin for himself in 1843. He tried to build a medieval house, but it looks profoundly Victorian: like hundreds of mid-nineteenth-century parsonages. Despite the bargeboards on the gable end and the Gothic windows, it does not have the exuberance of later-Victorian middle-class houses.

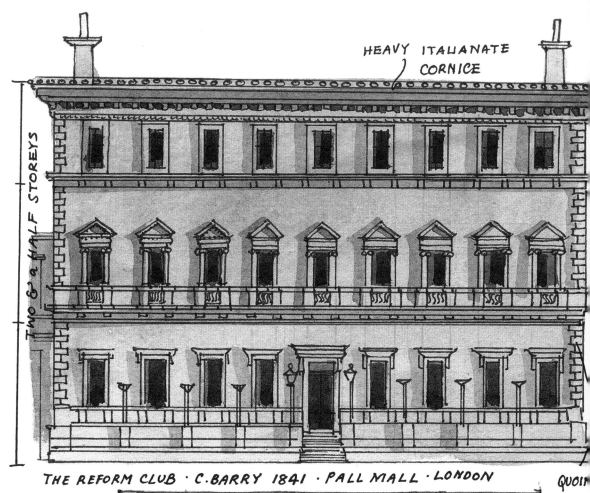

HEAVY ITALIANATE CORNICE

TWO & a HALF STOREYS

THE REFORM CLUB · C·BARRY 1841 · PALL MALL · LONDON

QUOIN

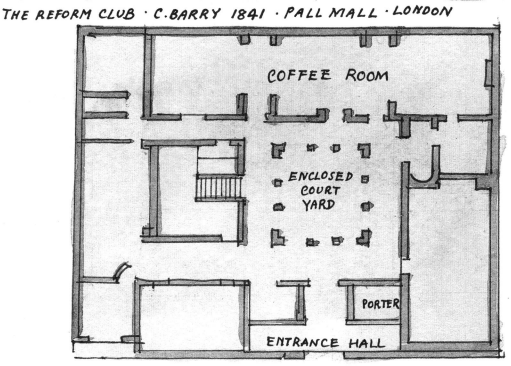

COFFEE ROOM

ENCLOSED COURT YARD

PORTER

ENTRANCE HALL

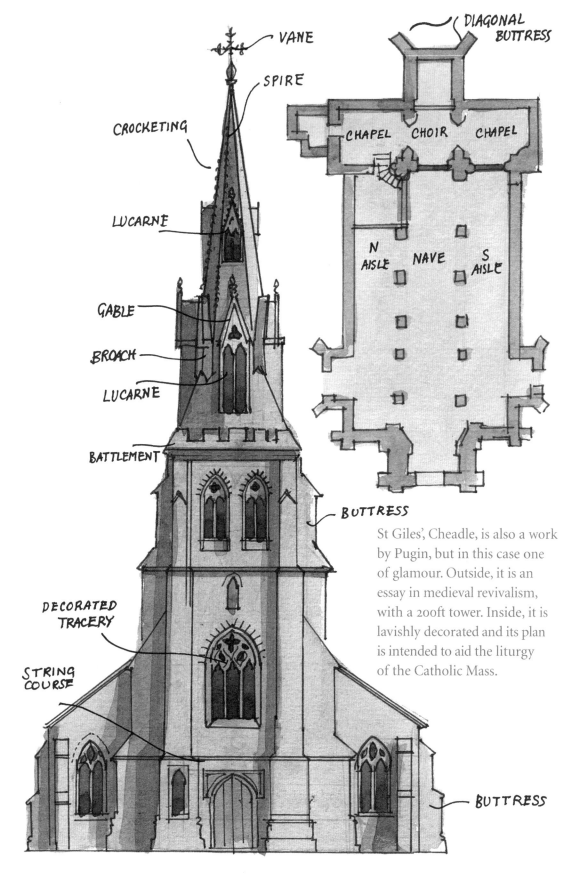

VANE

SPIRE

CROCKETING

LUCARNE

GABLE

BROACH

LUCARNE

BATTLEMENT

DECORATED
TRACERY

STRING
COURSE

DIAGONAL
BUTTRESS

CHAPEL   CHOIR   CHAPEL

N
AISLE   NAVE   S
AISLE

BUTTRESS

BUTTRESS

St Giles', Cheadle, is also a work
by Pugin, but in this case one
of glamour. Outside, it is an
essay in medieval revivalism,
with a 200ft tower. Inside, it is
lavishly decorated and its plan
is intended to aid the liturgy
of the Catholic Mass.

FRETTED BARGEBOARD

STOP

DEPRESSED ARCH

GREEK KEY ov FRET

rather Austere greek order

LOZEN

GOTHIC DOOR

TWO DOORWAYS beneath a common ENTABLATURE

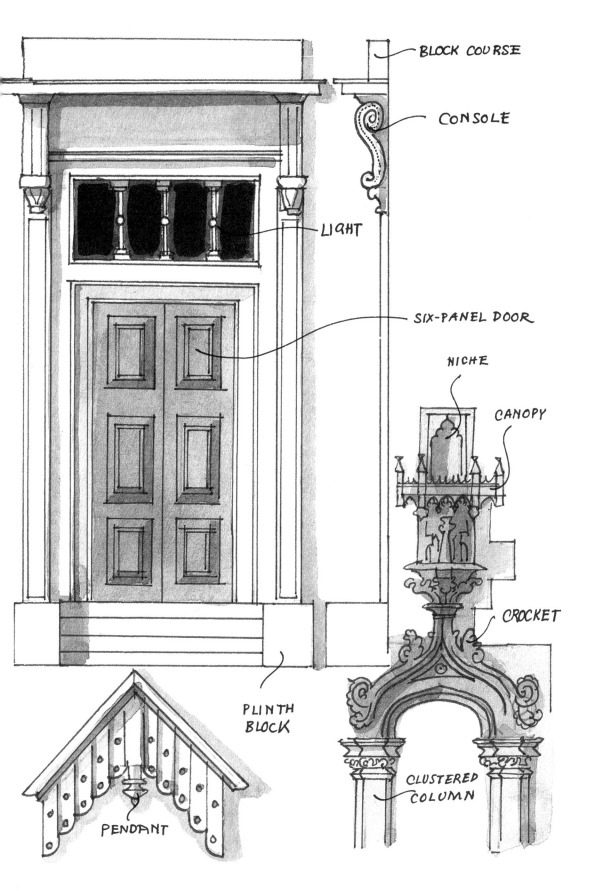

BLOCK COURSE

CONSOLE

LIGHT

SIX-PANEL DOOR

NICHE

CANOPY

CROCKET

PLINTH BLOCK

CLUSTERED COLUMN

PENDANT

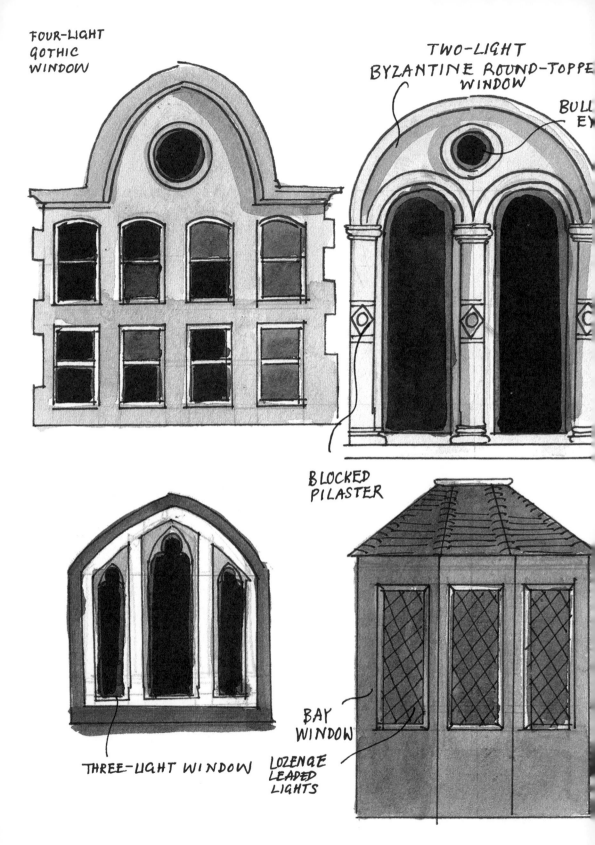

FOUR-LIGHT
GOTHIC
WINDOW

TWO-LIGHT
BYZANTINE ROUND-TOPPE
WINDOW

BULL
EY

BLOCKED
PILASTER

THREE-LIGHT WINDOW

BAY
WINDOW

LOZENGE
LEADED
LIGHTS

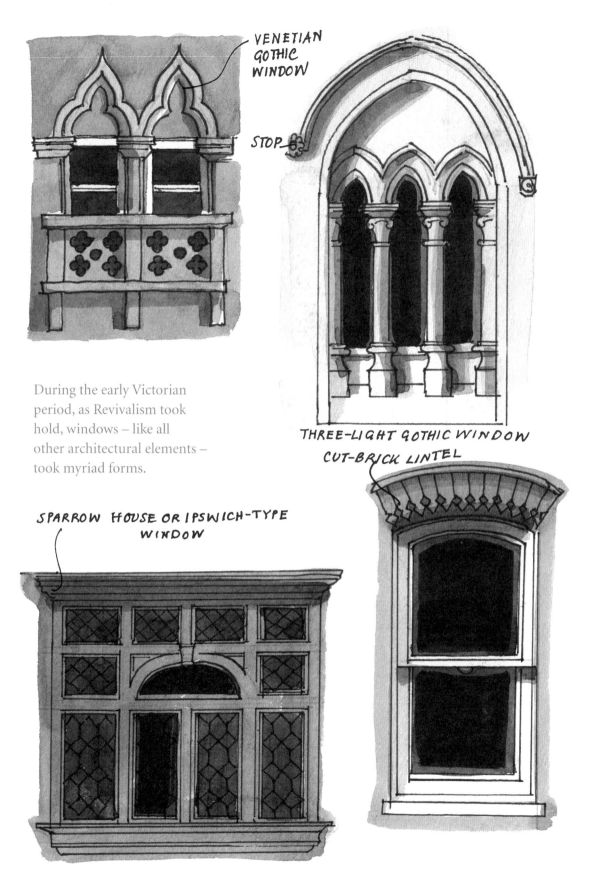

VENETIAN
GOTHIC
WINDOW

STOP

THREE-LIGHT GOTHIC WINDOW

CUT-BRICK LINTEL

During the early Victorian period, as Revivalism took hold, windows – like all other architectural elements – took myriad forms.

SPARROW HOUSE OR IPSWICH-TYPE WINDOW

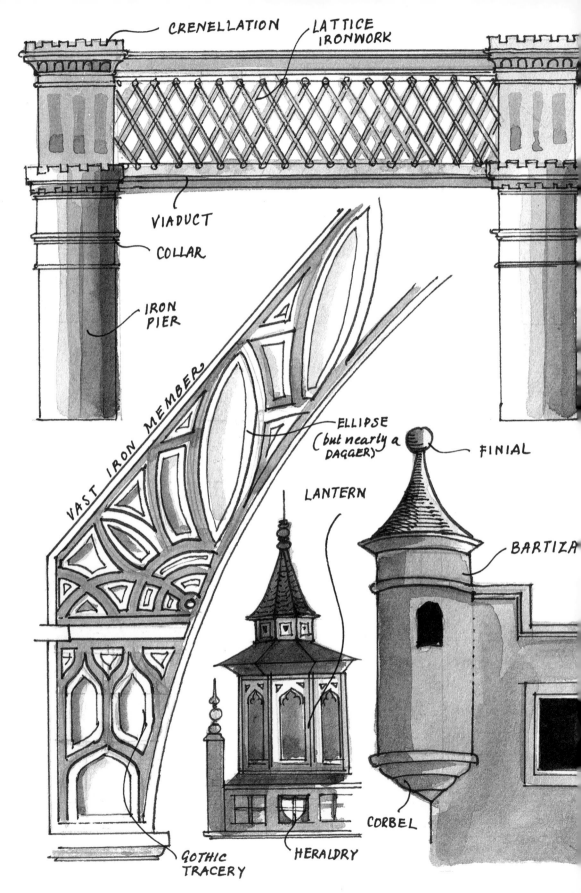

CRENELLATION

LATTICE IRONWORK

VIADUCT

COLLAR

IRON PIER

VAST IRON MEMBER

ELLIPSE
(but nearly a DAGGER)

FINIAL

LANTERN

BARTIZA

CORBEL

GOTHIC TRACERY

HERALDRY

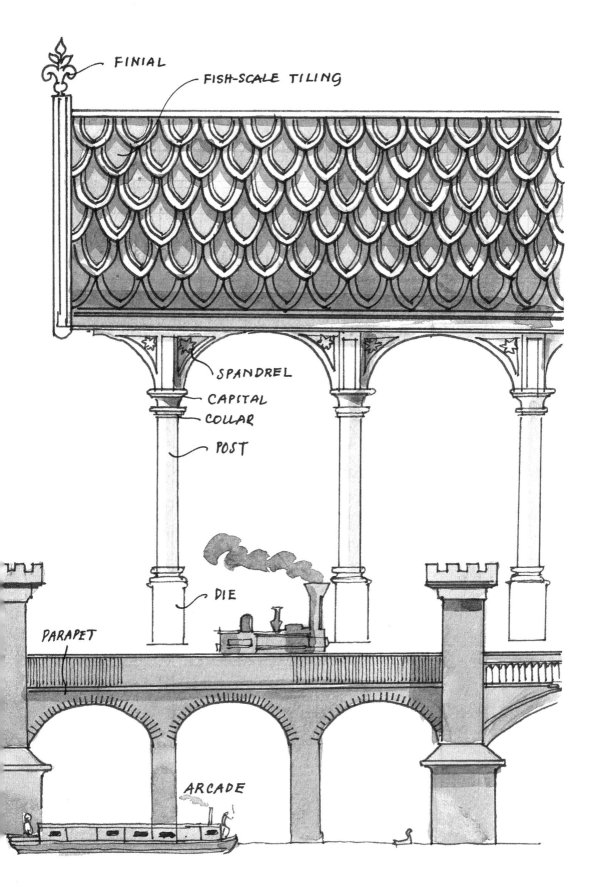

FINIAL

FISH-SCALE TILING

SPANDREL

CAPITAL

COLLAR

POST

DIE

PARAPET

ARCADE

The publication in 1849 and 1851 of *The Seven Lamps of Architecture* and *The Stones of Venice* were to have a dramatic effect on Gothic architecture. The author, JOHN RUSKIN (1819–1900), had travelled widely in Europe, particularly in Italy, where he had made a detailed study of the Gothic buildings of Venice and Verona. He was especially interested in the surface decoration of buildings, and produced almost photographically detailed watercolours of the Istrian limestone, marble, brick and rendering that make up the façades of Venice's *palazzos*. These studies were hugely influential, giving rise to the use of POLYCHROMY, the combination of stones and bricks of varying colours in the elevations of a building. This was to reach its apogee in Keble College, Oxford, built in 1867–83 by William Butterfield. Although Gothic in overall design, the college's striped, diapered and chequered patterns on simple and unarticulated elevations are quite unlike the plain stone or brick of Pugin or the early Victorian Gothic Revivalists.

Nor was Gothic the only style to be explored. The nineteenth century saw VENETIAN, ITALIANATE, BYZANTINE, NEO-CLASSICAL and NEO-RENAISSANCE designs carried out in domestic and ecclesiastical projects, often by the same architects. Charles Barry produced the Gothic Houses of Parliament in 1837–67, and the Italianate Reform Club in 1837–41. In the second half of the century, the barriers between these styles began to break down, and a free or eclectic version developed. A prime example of this is the Natural History Museum in South Kensington, designed by Alfred Waterhouse in 1873–81, in which Continental and English Gothic and Romanesque combine in a completely modern design. Its 650ft façade is not based on a cathedral or college format, but is an entirely new arrangement. It is built of brick, although much of the elevation is cased in terracotta, with Gothic, Byzantine and purely imaginative decorative elements, in this case animals and fossils. Inside, the walls are constructed of terracotta and polychrome brick, enclosing a steel-roofed courtyard.

The nineteenth century was the century of HUGE buildings. For the first time, the cathedrals of the Middle Ages were challenged in size. St Pancras Station and hotel or the Law Courts, built by G. E. Street in 1874–82, are simply bigger than anything that came before. In all Britain's new industrial towns, libraries, institutes, town halls and museums rose majestically in Gothic, Greek, Italianate, Baroque or neo-Classical styles, the choice often made by the donor. A High Church benefactor would favour Gothic, a Gradgrindian new-money industrialist or group of city fathers might prefer neo-Classical or, more fancifully, a Renaissance chateau, as in the bizarre Chateau Impney in Worcestershire, the wild folly of a Droitwich salt magnate. A building's style was chosen to represent the values of the institution it housed, or those with which the donor wished to be identified.

Another building type that assumed increasing importance was the SCHOOL. The Elementary Education Act of 1870 ignited a wildfire of school building throughout the country. Schools were, as was everything in Victorian Britain, built in all the popular styles, but in this case, there was a division. For the greater part, PUBLIC SCHOOLS adhered to the Gothic, an indication of the importance attached to religious education in such institutions. Dozens of neo-monastic complexes were built with refectories, libraries and a chapel. But in the newly important STATE sector, one of the two last great architectural movements of the nineteenth century became triumphant.

QUEEN ANNE, or Queen Anne Revival, was the name given to the work of a group of architects, many of whom had originally been Gothicists, who sought a new language for secular building. Rather than looking to medieval England, Europe, ancient Greece or Rome, these architects, including J. J. Stevenson, E. W. Godwin, Philip Webb, Basil Champneys and, perhaps most famously, Norman Shaw, turned instead to the domestic buildings of seventeenth- and early eighteenth-century England. This period, described by the aesthete Sacheverell Sitwell as the GOLDEN AGE of British architects and craftsmen, was perceived as being delicate and artistic, bringing to architecture the qualities of sweetness and light. The principal features of this revival were sash windows, often with thick and frequent glazing bars, brick pediments, either pointed or segmental, tall, visible chimney stacks and Dutch gables. Brick was the main building material, with some work picked out in stone. From the 1870s onwards, Queen Anne style was often adopted for domestic projects, none of which reproduce previous buildings. Indeed, despite the nomenclature, it is impossible to confuse these houses with those built during the actual reign of Queen Anne. Rather, they are a confection, an idiosyncratic grouping of architectural elements combined, significantly, asymmetrically.

Another Queen Anne architect, E. R. Robson, was put in charge of the new 'Board schools'. His influence remains visible today in the dozens of towering, be-gabled and heavily chimney-stacked schools, some still serving their original purpose, some converted to residential or other use. However, the Queen Anne style is at its happiest when used for houses. In 1876, the first properties were completed at Bedford Park in Chiswick, a utopian model village of huge houses for the aesthetically minded middle classes, built mainly by NORMAN SHAW (1831–1912). His designs are unlike any seen before, both in type and in detailing, with bay and bow-fronted windows, oriels, bull's eyes, dormers and gables, heavy cornices and covings, and rather dominating chimneys. In fact, so many details do they contain that these houses are in themselves a justification for an architectural primer.

As a young man, Shaw worked in the offices of G. E. Street, as did WILLIAM MORRIS (1834–96). With Philip Webb (1831–1915), Morris was a leading light of the ARTS AND CRAFTS MOVEMENT. A reaction to the accelerating industrialisation of Britain, this movement was a complete rejection of mechanised manufacturing. Morris and his followers believed that pre-industrial craftsmen, who had an innate knowledge of their trade and materials, produced artefacts of far greater intrinsic value than machine- or factory-made equivalents. They glorified the medieval mason's skills, and sought to rekindle those abilities. Morris & Co was established not only as an architectural firm, but also as the maker of all domestic goods, from the textiles and wallpapers with which the name is still associated to furniture and ironwork. The designs were of flowing line with sophisticated and varied sources of inspiration from as far afield as Japan. The Arts and Crafts movement continued in various forms until the Second World War, and its influence remains.

The greater part of Britain's TERRACED houses also date from this period, fulfilling the need created by speedy population growth. Such houses were usually unadorned, except for mass-produced decorative elements in cement or terracotta. With them came PUBS. These are often at the end of terraces and lavishly fitted with glazed and brightly coloured external ceramic decoration and sophisticated lettering. They use the same visual language of NEO-BAROQUE as the great theatres of Frank Matcham, such as the Coliseum and the London Hippodrome, which are heavy with swagging and ornate plasterwork.

The nineteenth century can be rather confusing, as the styles and fashions changed quickly, and sometimes ran contemporaneously. Most of them are a revival of a previous age, with the exception of the genuinely original and quirky Queen Anne style. But it is also a time of great INVENTIVENESS and unparalleled energy and creativity.

STRING COURSE

RIDGE

TWO-LIGHT WINDOW

FINIAL

The Museum of Natural
History, Oxford, was designed
by Benjamin Woodward in
1855. It is Gothic, in the style
of a Flemish town hall, but with
nods to Venice. It has wonderful
carving by James and John
O'Shea on the windows, and a
door depicting natural forms,
apt for a natural history museum.

PYRAMIDAL
ROOF

TOWER

PLATE TRACERY

LUCARNES

DORMERS

GOTHIC DOORWAY WITH FIGURATIVE CARVING

GATEHOUSE

OPEN &
BROKEN
PEDIMENT

DOME
TURRET
or
CUPOLA

DEPRESSED
ARCH

PILASTER

RED BRICK WITH
STONE DRESSINGS

CORONET

HERALDIC BEAST

STRAP

TURRET WITH CROWN

BADGE

CUSPING

NORMAN ARCH
(RUNDBOGENSTIL)

OPEN

BROKEN

EXAGGERATED KEYSTONE

OPEN & BROKEN
PEDIMENT

VENETIAN
GOTHIC
DOOR

LIGHT

FIELDED PANELS

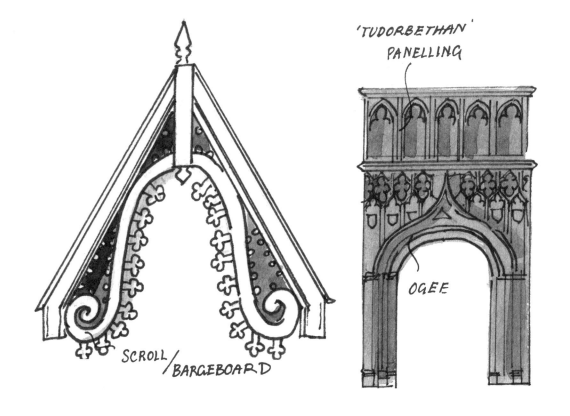

'TUDORBETHAN'
PANELLING

OGEE

SCROLL/BARGEBOARD

SWAGS IN TYMPANUM

GLAZED
DOOR

'ECLECTIC' ENTRANCE

ARCHITRAVE

FOUR-LIGHT SASH WINDOW
RUSTICATION

HEAVY PEDIMENT
WINDOW with
BALCONY

MOUCHETTE

DIE

NEO-GOTHIC WINDOW

VOLUTES

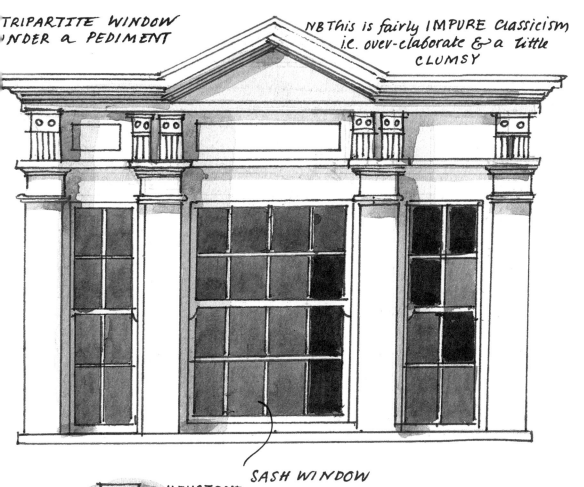

TRIPARTITE WINDOW UNDER a PEDIMENT

NB This is fairly IMPURE Classicism i.e. over-elaborate & a little CLUMSY

SASH WINDOW

KEYSTONE

VOUSSOIRS

BIFORA – TWO-ARCHED BYZANTINE WINDOW

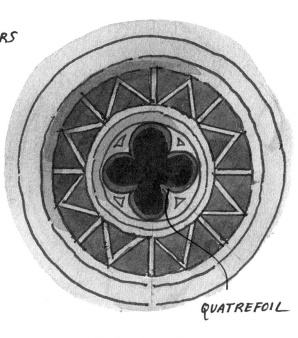

QUATREFOIL

WHEEL WINDOW

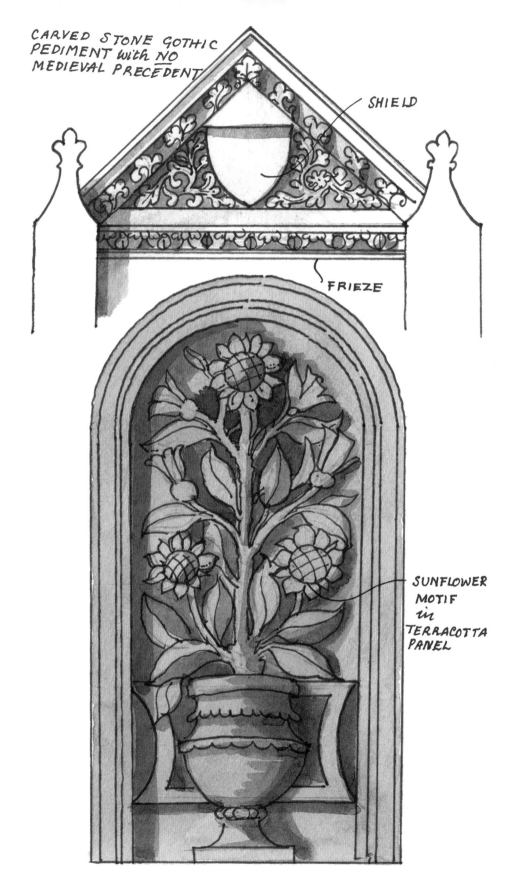

CARVED STONE GOTHIC PEDIMENT with NO MEDIEVAL PRECEDENT

SHIELD

FRIEZE

SUNFLOWER MOTIF in TERRACOTTA PANEL

SERPENTINE
BARGEBOARDS

CARVED DECORATION
IN GABLE END

OPEN
SEGMENTAL
PEDIMENT

SCROLL

BARONS
COURT

TERRACOTTA PANEL

FLUTED
PILASTER

1868

EDWARDIAN

If you want to move forward, you have to look back. That is the way with architecture, and it was never more true than in the EDWARDIAN period. This was the last decade in which all the many revivals continued to vie for the post of most suitable style for a new building.

Edward VII had spent an appallingly long time being Prince of Wales. He was sixty when his mother, Queen Victoria, died in 1901, and had been excluded from all affairs of State. While awaiting his accession, he had grown stout, and had been a lover of pleasures of all sorts: food, shooting and ladies. This sybaritic style of life was reflected in the architecture of his reign: flowing Gothic, lush Wrenaissance, glamorous Louis Quinze or bold, free-style Classicism and Baroque. Every style of architecture was trotted out for one last lap of honour before the world-shattering Great War brought to an end the easy-going luxuries and architectural fancies of the nineteenth century. All the styles had matured, and although some buildings are spiritless and blank, many are the logical conclusion of these styles.

Sennowe Hall in Norfolk was built for Thomas Cook, grandson of the founder of the eponymous travel agency. Relieved of the business by its lucrative sale, he engaged the Norwich architect George Skipper (1856–1948) to massively enlarge and remodel his house in 1905. This Skipper did energetically and with typical bravura GRAND GESTURES. Pedimented windows, colonnades, statues silhouetted on the skyline, a porte-cochère, swags and giant-order pilasters are massed together to dramatic effect. In 1913, Aston Webb (1849–1930) transformed Edward Blore's main front of BUCKINGHAM PALACE into an elaborately articulated façade that was as distinguished as its muscular and beefy neighbour, the Admiralty Arch of 1910.

At this time, all over Britain, generously proportioned and intricately detailed town halls, banks, swimming baths, pubs and theatres were being built with an imaginative sophistication and elaboration that had never been used before. It was a period that combined low wages, which allowed the best craftsmanship to be employed, with a generally high standard of drawing in the architect's office. This combination resulted in the creation of extraordinarily good MASONRY. Brickwork was also afforded great attention to detail. Small, handmade bricks and rubbed shaped bricks of the highest quality raised the thousands of banks built in the new suburbs to the level of minor masterpieces. Doorcases, windows and wooden cornicing were subject to the same attentions, and were made to so high a standard that many such buildings have even survived the subsequent century's depredations, which saw plastic fasciae and simplifications employed to make banking accessible. Even now, when once-dignified banking halls echo to the clatter of drinking office workers, the sheer HIGH QUALITY of the buildings remains dominant.

Although the scrolled pediment and the dentilated cornice ruled the public buildings of the high street, another style altogether was gently but firmly transforming DOMESTIC architecture. The ARTS AND CRAFTS MOVEMENT was not an Edwardian development, but instead, as mentioned in the previous chapter, was born to the Gothic Revival, and was a strapping middle-aged man of forty-five at the peak of his powers by the time Edward VII came to the throne. Central to the architectural thinking of the movement's founders, William Morris and Philip Webb, was an interest in the ENGLISH VERNACULAR. The vernacular in architecture means the local language of building, using local materials and working within a local tradition of building methods that reflect local conditions. True vernacular buildings are put up without the input of an architect, and their form may change over only a short distance, according to how the available stone or the economic conditions vary.

The vernacular school of thought was parent to the QUEEN ANNE REVIVAL (see page 146), and ran parallel to that great and inventive style in the hands of the second generation of practitioners, WILLIAM LETHABY (1857–1931), CHARLES VOYSEY (1857–1941), famous for his trademark broad eaves, and E. S. PRIOR (1852–1932).

Voewood in Norfolk was designed by Prior in 1903–05, and epitomises the mature style. Its plan is in the form of a butterfly to catch the health-promoting rays of the sun, a thought that would have been repugnant to a builder thirty years before. It is an essay in the VERNACULAR REVIVAL, and is very typical of the style in that it is a theoretical vernacular only. Buildings constructed in this form look like no others in the vicinity, or indeed anywhere else. Before work on Voewood began, the site was excavated to provide the sand and gravel that would become the two principal components of the concrete shell of the building. Also present were flint pebbles, which became one of the many materials that form the surface treatment of the house. Almost every other stone found anywhere in East Anglia gets a look-in, including carstone, chalk and knapped flint. The fine brickwork is the only material not sourced fairly locally.

The memorial library at Bedales School in Hampshire is an even more extreme example of the Arts and Crafts movement. It was designed and built by ERNEST GIMSON (1864–1919), and was constructed on a frame of green oak. The massive members were sawn by hand in a pit dug in the orchard just in front of the site, and the trusses they became are the dominant element in the building. Cracks that are large enough to put a hand inside do not affect the strength of the structure, and the warm oak and elm interior remains one of the best Arts and Crafts rooms in Britain.

The towering name of English Edwardianism is that of EDWIN LUTYENS (1869–1944). His varied work is sometimes monolithic, as at Lindisfarne Castle in Northumberland, which seems to grow from the living rock; sometimes in a stylish and assimilated vernacular, as at Overstrand Hall in Norfolk; and at other times sophisticated and monumental, as in his imperial apotheosis of the great Viceregal

Lodge in Delhi (1912–31), where neo-Classicism absorbs elements of Mughal and Hindu architecture in a final flourish of the BRITISH EMPIRE. Lutyens's work encompassed gardens, often in partnership with GERTRUDE JEKYLL (1843–1932), or larger city plans, as in the great avenues of New Delhi.

Meanwhile, in Glasgow, the idiosyncratic Scottish architect CHARLES RENNIE MACKINTOSH (1868–1928) had completed the Glasgow School of Art. This mannered and very personal combination of massive, dour Scottish BARONIAL and aesthetic JAPONAISERIE combines the most unlikely decorative elements bound together with sinuous ART NOUVEAU ironwork. In general, the flowing, fantastical Art Nouveau style was not a great success in Britain, or, at any rate, not to the extent that saw it adopted so freely in France, for example on the grand Paris Métro, or by the Vienna Secession.

Equivalents in ebullience, although not in the exaggerated use of the natural form that characterises that style, are the Whitechapel Art Gallery and Westminster Cathedral. The former was designed in 1899 by Charles Harrison Townsend (1851–1928). It is a genuinely peculiar building, as odd as any French Art Nouveau shop front, but drawing heavily on the vocabulary of Wren and the ENGLISH TRADITION. When building Westminster Cathedral between 1894 and 1902, on the other hand, J. Francis Bentley (1839–1902) trawled new waters for inspiration for his design. In this case, the BYZANTINE churches of Constantinople and the Levant provided a historical precedent for the striking polychrome façade that is obscured by the boorish and brutal modernism of Victoria Street.

The outbreak of the Great War in 1914 ended this luxurious age of architectural maundering. As the enormities of that conflict fanned the flames of social unrest and the Labour Party, so the first cool flickers of MODERNISM, either in the style's pure form or filtered through the rose-tinted spectacles of ART DECO, made their first appearance…

ATTENUATED
SHAPED GABLE

DELLA ROBBIA
TONDO
*This is actually
in Florence.
but is shown to
illustrate THE SOURCE
Of the design...*

ROYAL AR

BANDED TRUMEAU

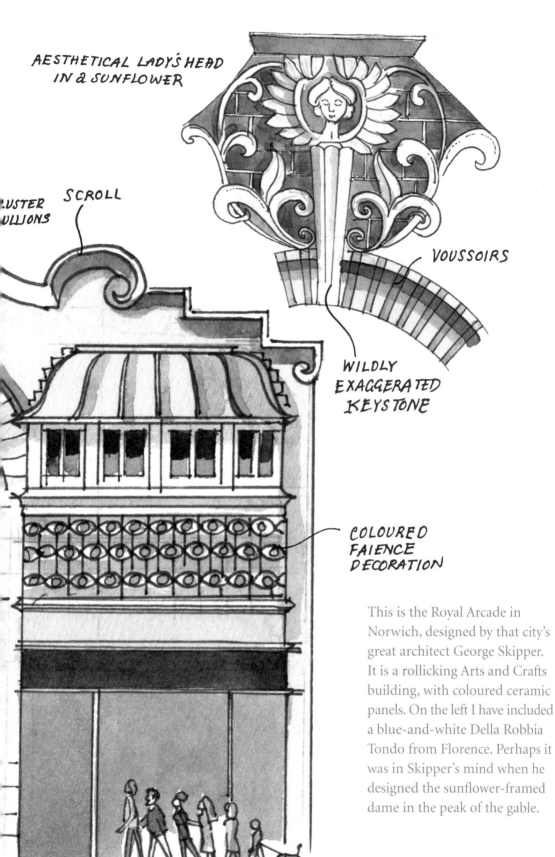

AESTHETICAL LADY'S HEAD
IN a SUNFLOWER

CLUSTER
MULLIONS

SCROLL

VOUSSOIRS

WILDLY
EXAGGERATED
KEYSTONE

COLOURED
FAIENCE
DECORATION

This is the Royal Arcade in Norwich, designed by that city's great architect George Skipper. It is a rollicking Arts and Crafts building, with coloured ceramic panels. On the left I have included a blue-and-white Della Robbia Tondo from Florence. Perhaps it was in Skipper's mind when he designed the sunflower-framed dame in the peak of the gable.

POLYGONAL CHIMNEY STACK

DIAPERED BRICKWORK

NEO-VERNACULAR USE OF MULTIFARIOUS MATERIALS

LOGGIA

WING

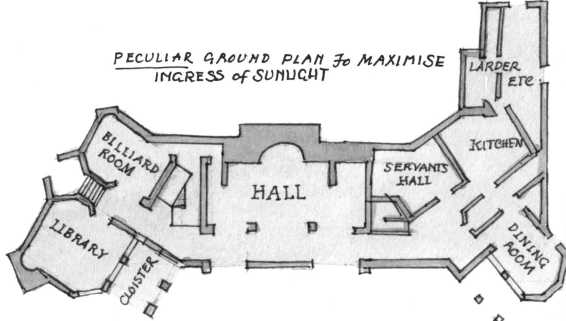

PECULIAR GROUND PLAN TO MAXIMISE INGRESS OF SUNLIGHT

BILLIARD ROOM

LARDER ETC

KITCHEN

SERVANTS HALL

HALL

LIBRARY

CLOISTER

DINING ROOM

The extraordinary ground plan of Voewood, Norfolk, built by E. S. Prior in 1905, throws out all the order of domestic architecture with the 'Butterfly Plan'. Opposite is Charles Rennie Mackintosh's Glasgow Art School, an equally revolutionary building of 1909.

STAIR WINDOW

TURRET

TALL STUDIO WINDOW

SEGMENTAL PEDIMENT

ARTIST at Work

PIER

OVERTHROW

FESTOON

SCROLLED
PEDIMENT

BLOCKED
ARCHITRAVE

BLOCK

PLINTH BLOCK

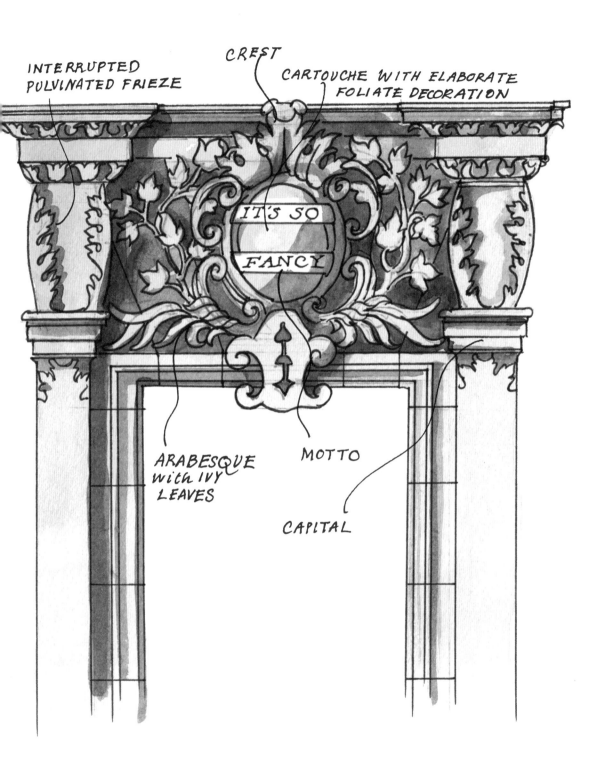

INTERRUPTED
PULVINATED FRIEZE

CREST

CARTOUCHE WITH ELABORATE
FOLIATE DECORATION

IT'S SO
FANCY

ARABESQUE
with IVY
LEAVES

MOTTO

CAPITAL

KEYSTONE

BLOCK

LOBED
ARCHITRAVE, the TOP & BOTTOM
SIDES
SEGMENTAL

INTERLOCKING
IRONGRILLE

SCROLLED
KEYSTONE

BAROQUE ARCHITRAVE

BULL'S
EYE

SWAG

OCTAGONAL BULL'S EYE

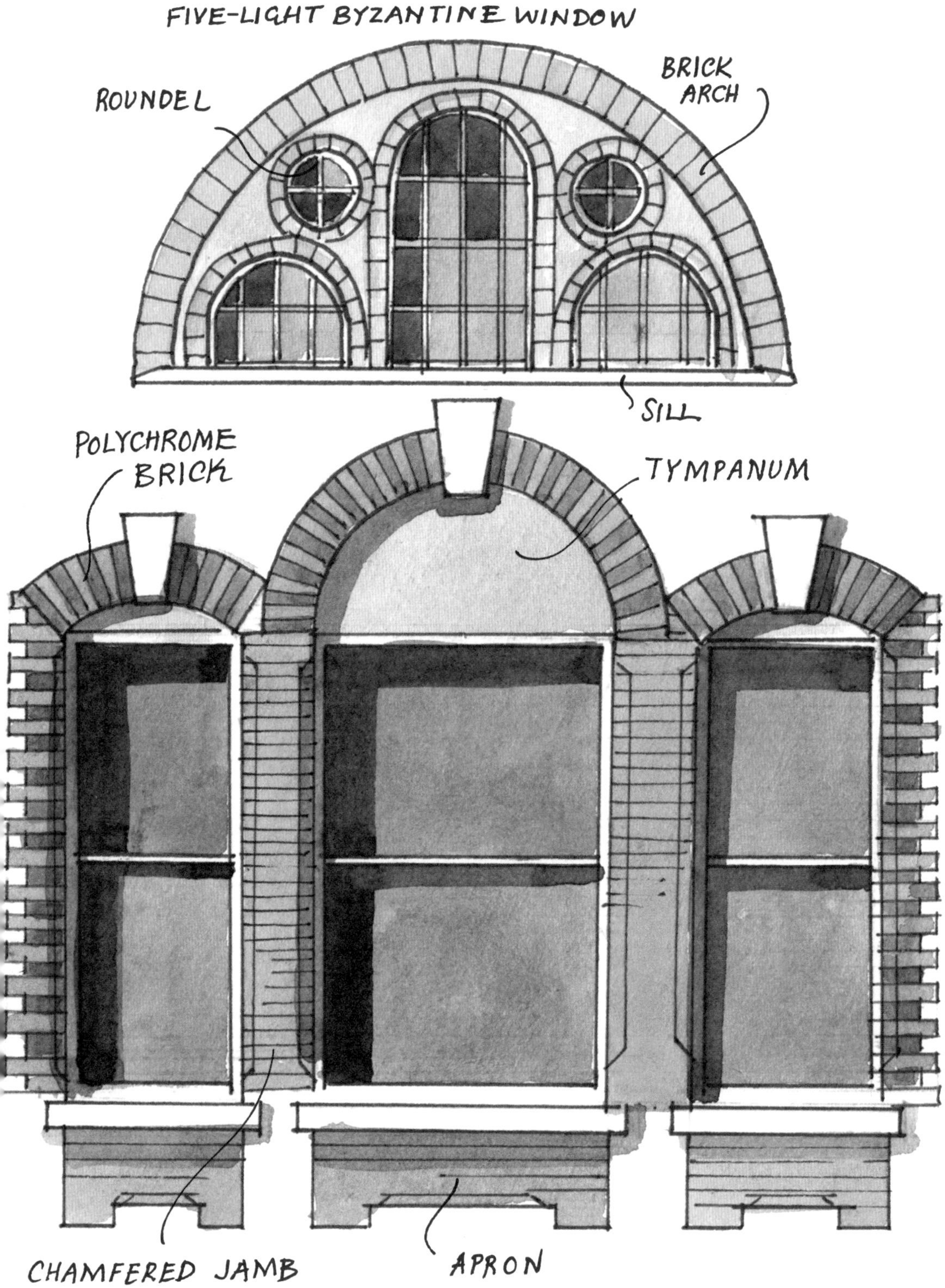

FIVE-LIGHT BYZANTINE WINDOW

ROUNDEL

BRICK ARCH

SILL

POLYCHROME BRICK

TYMPANUM

CHAMFERED JAMB

APRON

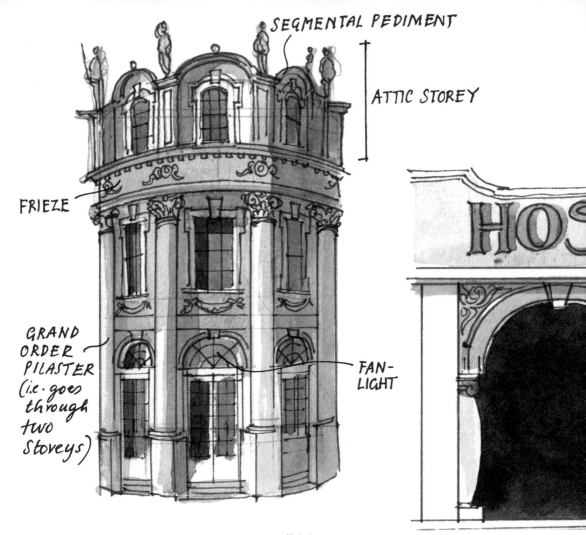

SEGMENTAL PEDIMENT

ATTIC STOREY

FRIEZE

GRAND ORDER PILASTER (i.e. goes through two stoveys)

FAN-LIGHT

HOS

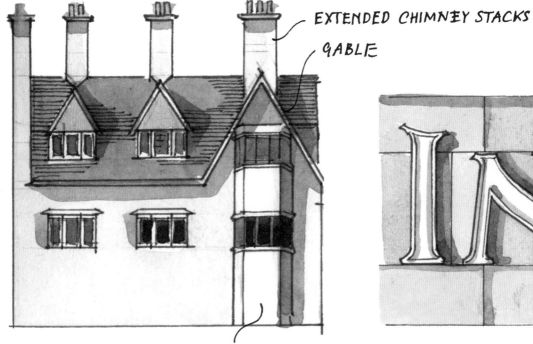

EXTENDED CHIMNEY STACKS

GABLE

TWO-STOREY BAY

IN

PEDIMENT (OF ODD PROFILE...)

THE
ROYAL
~TAL FOR CHILDREN

BALUSTER COLUMN

SPANDREL

INNERED ART NOUVEAU LETTERING on TERRACOTTA FRIEZE

...TITUTE

A NEW START in architecture is rare. Normally, a style develops gradually, morphing into its successor building by building. The arrival of the Normans in 1066, Inigo Jones's new Palladian style of the early seventeenth century and Pugin's Gothic Revival are exceptions. And so was MODERNISM. It was not home-grown, and it is perhaps partly because of its alien status as a German import that it has never been taken fully to the heart of the English housebuilder.

Beginning with the revolution-fuelled Constructivists in Soviet Russia and in Germany, the Modernist movement found its clearest expression in the Bauhaus (1919–1933) through the 1920s and '30s. Run by three giants, WALTER GROPIUS (1883–1969), HANS 'HANNES' MEYER (1889–1954) and LUDWIG MIES VAN DER ROHE (1886–1969), this Weimar institution set out as a school of architecture as well as industrial, graphic, textile and ceramic design. Its output combined the utopian simplicity of the Arts and Crafts movement with the clean lines of Constructivism.

Modernism, with its cool, geometric and undecorated lines, was a product of early twentieth-century Germany. A decade before, the AEG Turbine Factory of 1909 (Peter Behrens, 1868–1940) was one of the country's earliest buildings in the new style, but the hard, elegant lines of the industrial quickly spread to the residential.

The closure of the Bauhaus in 1933 against the backdrop of Hitler's profound disapproval (he saw the school as hotching with Communists and Jews) led to a diaspora of its architects and designers to England and the US. Serious Modernist architects began working in England from then on. ERICH MENDELSOHN (1887–1953, a German Jew) and SERGE CHERMAYEFF (1900–1996, a Russian Jew) built the De La Warr Pavilion in Bexhill-on-Sea, East Sussex, in 1935, bringing the cool simple lines of this style to the genteel south coast, while a smaller but equally elegant and spare building, the Penguin Pool at London Zoo (sadly now abandoned by its Antarctic tenants in favour of less architecturally distinguished surroundings) is the work of BERTHOLD LUBETKIN (1901–1990, again a Russian Jew).

The last building to become the home of the Bauhaus looked like a factory itself, with its concrete and glass elevations and curtain walling. It was the work carried out here, which was further inspired by the Dutch De Stijl paintings of Piet Mondrian, that established this rectangular straitjacket of twentieth-century building. Decoration of any sort was forbidden, and no reference to any styles of architecture from previous ages was entertained. Indeed, such considerations were perceived as bourgeois and reactionary. A truncated architectural vocabulary was needed to describe this new style, the characterisics of which were flat roofs, white concrete, strong geometric lines, cantilevered balconies, copious use of glass, and a COMPLETE ABSENCE OF DECORATION.

LE CORBUSIER (1887–1965) was a devoted and polemic Modernist. His reduction of a house to a '*machine à habiter*' aimed to make decoration or historical reference redundant; he believed that there was a solution to everything and that ORDER could be the natural state of things. His administrative buildings in Chandigarh in India, for example, were planned for a brave new world order, but the years have cloaked them in glossy mango trees and covered them with the accretions of India, surrounding them with shanty towns, donkeys and gloomy camels. Now they look nothing like the architect's schematic drawings.

Sir John Summerson, in his essay *The Case for a Theory of Modern Architecture* (1957), says of Modernism: 'It would be difficult to show that this complex of architecture and ideas is anything short of valid in relation to present-day conditions. There is indeed no other complex of forms and ideas which seriously rivals it.' Summerson was the champion of CLASSICISM and saviour of Georgian London, and even he felt that Modernism was the architecture of the future, carried away by the optimism of the 1950s.

The English were, and remain, resistant to the rather hectoring ways of Modernism, including the overbearing insistence on its ability to morally improve the inhabitants of its bleak new housing. They were also oblivious to the not-unstylish spare beauty of its buildings, its economy of line and its dynamic asymmetry, and looked for more.

ART DECO, the superficial and glitzy style of the cinemas, plugged the gap. The rise of the cinema and the Jazz Age were in some ways the antidote to Modernism, being sensual, sybaritic and free-ranging. Decorative elements from Egypt were also rolled into this eclectic style, spawned by Howard Carter's discovery of the grave of Tutankhamun in 1922. The MOVIE HOUSE became the same sort of focus for architectural attention as the church or the country house in previous centuries. Initially, cinemas were designed to seem as close to refined Louis XIV interiors as possible, in an effort to lure middle-class customers to what were perceived as unsavoury fleapits. D. W. Griffith's film *Intolerance* (1916) was not a commercial success, but its sets were a phenomenon. That depicting the court of Nebuchadnezzar in ancient Babylon was the largest film set ever built, and was constructed by builders and plasterers who had travelled from Italy for the 1915 San Francisco World's Fair. Inspired by this set, the showmen Charles Toberman (1880–1981) and Sid Grauman (1879–1950) built the EGYPTIAN THEATRE in Hollywood in 1922. It had a colonnaded portico on top of which an actor dressed as an Egyptian marched back and forth firing a gun to announce the start of the next show.

Developments as lurid as this could not fail to cross the Atlantic, and within ten years similar cinemas were being built in Britain, often adorned with giant Egyptian or Greek or even oriental exteriors.

This jolly style was used in a diluted form for other, newer building forms: the garage, the bus station and the department store.

A second icon of the early twentieth century was the OCEAN LINER. Modern and luxurious, the Cunard or P&O ships epitomised everything that felt good. During the economic depression that gripped the world after the Wall Street Crash of 1929 until the outbreak of the Second World War ten years later, these magnificent vessels symbolised an unfailing and much-needed optimism. The ships' form – the horizontal emphasis broken by the strong vertical of the chimneys – is echoed in many buildings of the period.

Whether early-twentieth-century architectural style was derived from Cunard liners or from the new technology of the RADIO (Chermayeff also designed radio cases), it gives rise to a strange question. Eighty years on, is the difference between hardline and austere MODERNISM and the jaunty and light-hearted ART DECO so very clear? Or have they fused together into what is, after all, only a style, and not a complete and timeless architectural panacea?

The Art Deco style was further diluted for domestic use and, together with a bowdlerised Modernism, pops up in most rows of assorted cheap villas lining Britain's new arterial roads. Osbert Lancaster, the cartoonist, architectural historian and social columnist, christened such developments BYPASS VARIEGATED. These houses, more than any other buildings, characterise twentieth-century Britain, from debased, mock-Tudor terraces to modernistic blocks, despite their being customised and defaced with mock-Georgian doors. Such chirpy, rendered villas with their bow fronts often use the ubiquitous metal-framed CRITTALL WINDOW. These painted frames were long-lasting, due to being galvanised by hot-dipping, and were developed using a technology devised for the manufacture of ammunition boxes in the Great War. The ability to make them follow a curve has had an enduring effect on twentieth-century Britain.

The public architecture of the later years of the century is still basically MODERN in style, despite sallies into neo-Classicism, neo-vernacular and the desperate, specious dead end of post-modernism. Throughout the 1950s and '60s, architects working in a pared-down vocabulary explored the geometry of horizontal and vertical straight lines and, for visual dynamics, relied upon the shadows cast or the repeated alternating of glass and wall.

The 1970s ushered in BRUTALISM. The nomenclature is self-explanatory, and the style relied on the use of preformed steel and concrete components, often of a very gritty mix. At the National Theatre on London's South Bank, Sir Denys Lasdun (1914–2001) worked in shuttered concrete with the grain of the shuttering adding an unlikely natural form, at least in two dimensions. Sir Hugh Casson's Elephant House, again at London Zoo, uses concrete to echo the creased and wrinkled hides of its tenants (they also have moved to more contemporary accommodation and the pachyderm complex now houses a few warthogs as undistinguished squatters). Two giants of the late twentieth and early twenty-first centuries are Sir Norman Foster (born 1935) and Lord Rogers (born 1933). Rogers designed the Lloyd's building in the City of London, a new kind of tower block that wears its pants outside its trousers, and the 'Gherkin', Foster's skyline improvement to the Square Mile, is a new take on the Chrysler building in New York. DECONSTRUCTURALISM, the emperor's new architectural clothes as espoused by Enric Miralles' Scottish Parliament or Sir Terry Farrell's The Deep on the banks of the River Humber, involves taking an already charmless building to pieces and sticking the bits together again in an unconvincing way.

Nevertheless, these recent wild feats of engineering, with tensile structures of architectural textiles, implausibly massive sheets of glass and parabolic curves of steel, have completely changed the look of large buildings, and have introduced a sense of humour and FUN that Modernism occasionally missed. Whether the fevered outbreak of towers in London over the last ten years will be seen to have improved the city remains to be seen; the Shard, so tall its elegant top is often wreathed in cloud, is already a well-loved component of the skyline, but perhaps the relentless regiment of commercial blocks that face Sir Charles Barry's Palace of Westminster, Norman Shaw's Scotland Yard and the Tate Modern may seem to have been a short-term gain only.

Buildings until recently despised as featureless and invasive have become of increasing interest to architecture students and the building-loving public. Just as the unloved Victorian architects found their champion in the poet Sir John Betjeman, who saved St Pancras railway station from destruction in 1967 after several decades in the shade, so the best of twentieth-century architecture is taking its rightful place in the canon of architectural history.

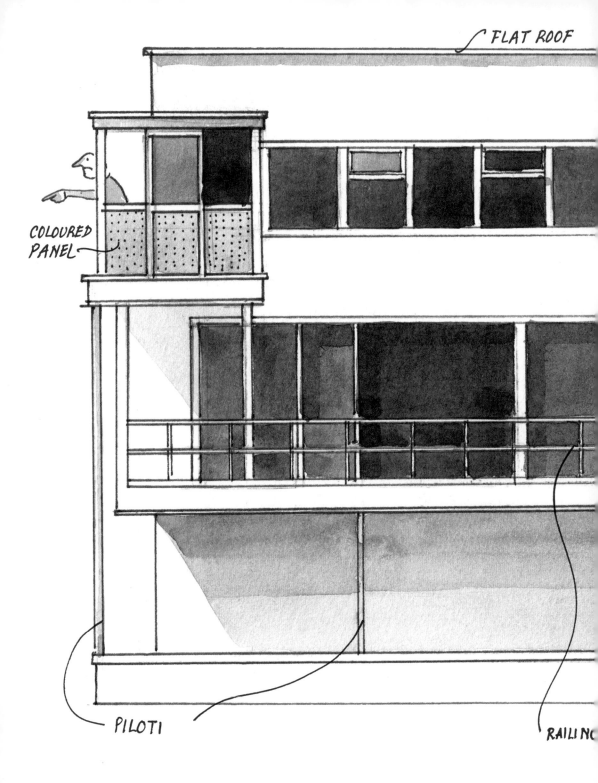

FLAT ROOF

COLOURED
PANEL

PILOTI

RAILING

POODLE GLAZED WALL BALCONY GARAGE

There are very few details to describe here – but after all, that's what Modernism is all about: clean lines and proportion.

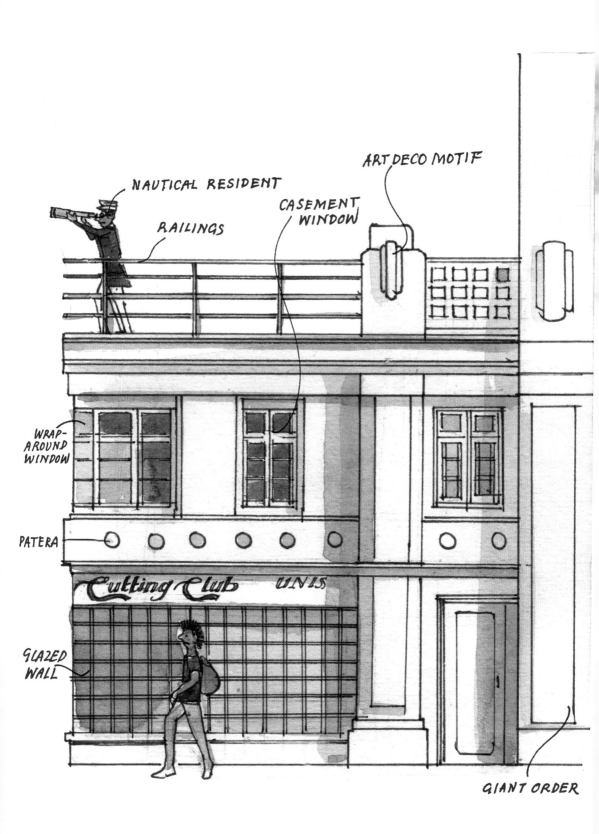

NAUTICAL RESIDENT

RAILINGS

CASEMENT WINDOW

ART DECO MOTIF

WRAP-AROUND WINDOW

PATERA

GLAZED WALL

Cutting Club UNIS

GIANT ORDER

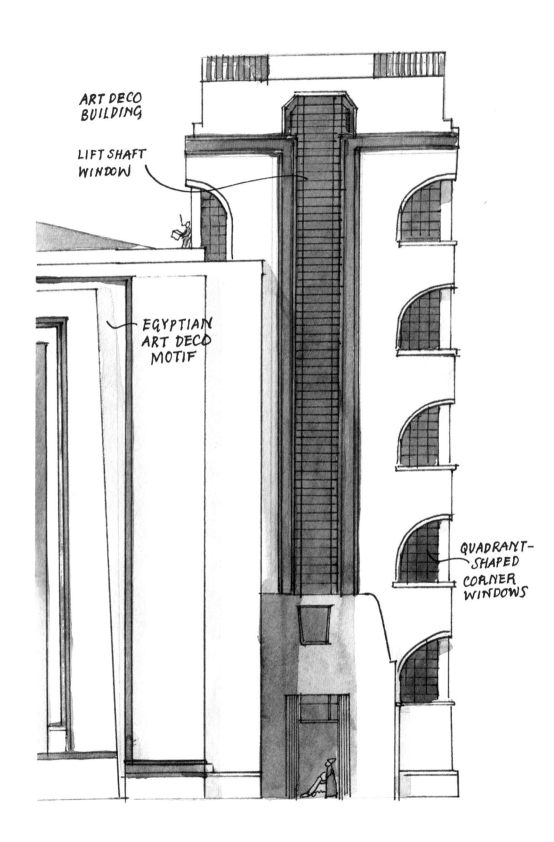

ART DECO
BUILDING

LIFT SHAFT
WINDOW

EGYPTIAN
ART DECO
MOTIF

QUADRANT-
SHAPED
CORNER
WINDOWS

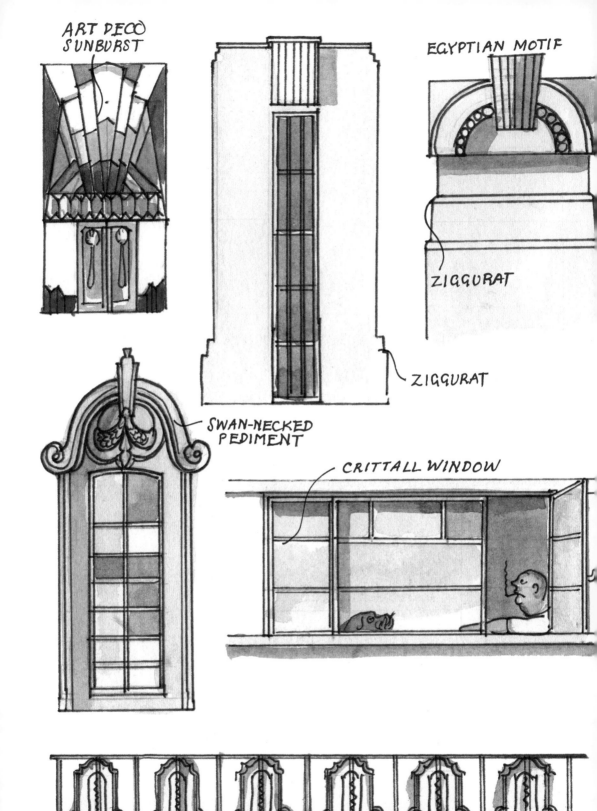

ART DECO
SUNBURST

EGYPTIAN MOTIF

ZIGGURAT

ZIGGURAT

SWAN-NECKED
PEDIMENT

CRITTALL WINDOW

ART DECO LOUIS XIV RAILING

FASCIA

PILOTI

TIME TABLE

PARAPET

RAINWATER OUTLET

CONCRETE SHUTTERING

MODULAR BUILDING

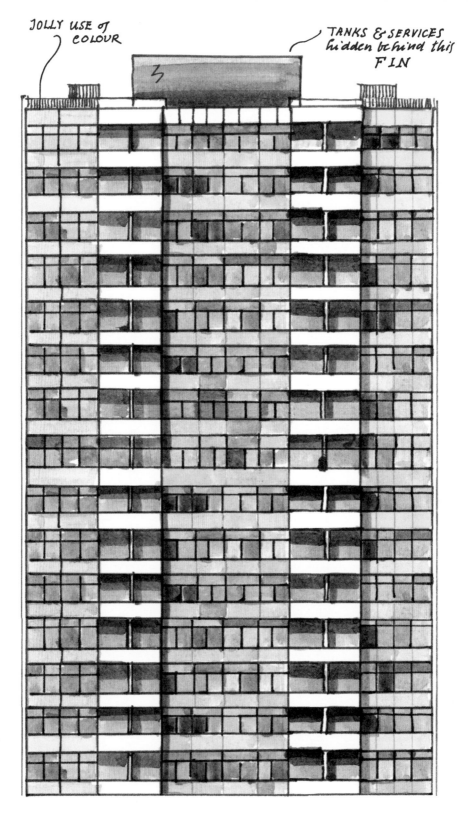

JOLLY USE OF COLOUR

TANKS & SERVICES hidden behind this FIN

GOLDEN LANE ESTATE · CHAMBERLIN, POWELL & BON 1953-'63 · Formal grid & ADORED by Modernists

GEORGE THOMSON BUILDING·CORPUS CHRISTI COLLEGE·CAMBRIDGE.
PHILIP DOWSON ASSOC' 1963-4 ·BOLD GEOMETRIC FORMS ~ Does this
feel like a CLASSICAL building? Even without CLASSICAL detail?
a contemporary CLOISTER...

The ELEPHANT HOUSE, London Zoo. CASSON CONDER
PARTNERSHIP. Deep grooves in the walls reminiscent
of elephants' WRINKLED SKIN & the ROOFS of a group
of ANIMALS. Symbolic Concrete Expressionism 1962

BIG SUNNY WINDOWS to let in a NEW DAWN

PRE~FAB on the EXCALIBUR ESTATE, BELLINGHAM. Uniseco
ltd 1945. DREAM HOMES for the BOMBED OUT. 11 Companies
built these post~war FACTORY~MADE Bungalows. Built to
LAST 5-10 years... SEVERAL SURVIVE TODAY

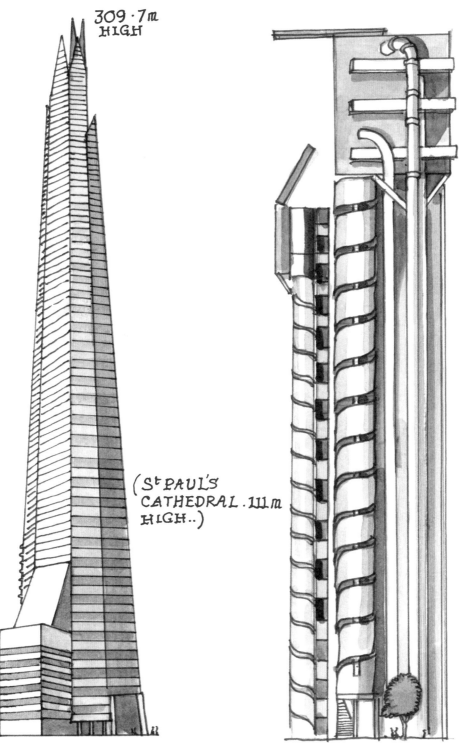

309·7m
HIGH

(St PAUL'S
CATHEDRAL·111m
HIGH..)

THE SHARD·2009-12
RENZO PIANO. The last word
in BOLD statements...?

THE LLOYD'S BUILDING·RICHARD
ROGERS. 1981·86·heavy articulation
& every function visible·very Gothic

ARCHETYPES

Few buildings are dreamt up from scratch. Even the most outlandish architectural projects have a PRECEDENT. Often that precedent is hard to identify and sometimes the architect starts work with the roughest of sketches that seem like pure geometry. However, nobody works in a vacuum and at any point in architectural history there have always been inspirational models. These are the buildings that have so defined a style or a solution to a practical problem that they become the conscious or unconscious focus of architects' thinking. Some are near UNIVERSAL in their significance.

A most obvious example is the Parthenon. This ARCHETYPAL Greek temple, built in 450BC, memorably situated on the Acropolis of Athens, looks down on Homer's wine-dark sea more than 2,500 years later. Through much of that time the Parthenon has been the model for subsequent buildings. Some are faithful copies, like that in Atlanta, Georgia, while others take modest liberties. The National Monument of Scotland, built by Charles Cockerell and William Playfair in Edinburgh in 1826, was intended to be a reproduction, but limited funds meant only a section was completed. The Choragic Monument of Lysicrates, amazingly preserved at the foot of the Acropolis in Athens, is used as the model for the 1831 memorial temple to the Scottish philanthropist Dugald Stewart, also in Edinburgh. At this time, the city was dubbed the ATHENS OF THE NORTH for its intellectual and academic reputation, so architectural quotation emphasised the Scottish capital's credentials and reputation. Similarly the Colosseum, the Pantheon and Trajan or Constantine's Arch make ancient Rome a FAMILY ALBUM OF WESTERN ARCHITECTURE. Distinguished ancestors of public buildings from the Pacific to the steppes of Russia have remained visible to Grand Tourists from the sixteenth century to the present day.

ALBERT SPEER (1905–1981), the favourite architect of Hitler's Thousand-Year Reich, built his own colosseum in Nuremberg in 1937 and his Nuremberg rally ground is a visualisation of an ancient hippodrome. Speer was conscious of the degree to which using these Roman models implied vast imperial power. He also conceived the idea of RUIN VALUE; again an homage to the way the architecture of the ancient world is seen in later centuries. Paris has a reproduction of the Pantheon built in 1758 and London had another copy of the first-century-AD Roman giant, dating from 1772 but now demolished and the site of Marks & Spencer's on Oxford Street. Napoleon, an emperor personally decked in SYMBOLS OF THE ROMAN EMPIRE, initiated work on a commemorative temple dedicated to his triumphant army. It was designed by Pierre-Alexandre Vignon (1763–1828). Events following his subsequent fall meant that in due course this was consecrated as the church of the Madeleine, Paris, in 1842. It is based on the Maison Carrée in Nîmes, one of the best-preserved buildings of the Empire and deeply symbolic of Bonaparte's vision of a French-dominated Europe.

Architects and architecturally literate Grand Tourists recorded the emerging ruins of the Roman Empire. All Classical architects have used details, windows, doorcases and the specific orders of different temples, theatres, baths and basilica in their work since the Renaissance. Vitruvius's four books of architecture were the first-century-AD written accompaniment to the stones. Later architects Palladio, Longhena, Alberti and Bramante themselves created archetypes and models. Andrea Palladio created new forms both in the double temple-fronted Venetian churches and the villas of the Veneto. These were deeply admired throughout the Western world. The Villa Capra or Villa Rotunda outside the northern Italian city of Vicenza was rebuilt in Britain in varying degrees of verisimilitude two centuries later at Mereworth in Kent, was all but recreated at Chiswick, London by Lord Burlington in 1729, and got a twentieth-century reworking in 1984 at Henbury Hall in Cheshire. The Villa Emo found an English life at Stourhead in Wiltshire, while the Villa Cornaro was the model for Marble Hill House in Twickenham, London, and also for Monticello, Thomas Jefferson's house in Virginia. The use of the Palladian archetype was in all these examples an expression of the builder's credentials as a forward-thinking ENLIGHTENMENT FIGURE.

In the seventeenth and eighteenth centuries, long-distance travel to Italy was blighted on one side by pirates in the Mediterranean and on the other by a series of precarious mountain passes across the Alps, which involved Swiss chair-carriers taking the young aristocratic Grand Tourists into the warm south in sedan chairs supported on their shoulders. But dangerous and expensive travel was not a *sine qua non* for those hungry for the new architectural ideas of the Renaissance. Palladio and the other great architects' designs were drawn and reproduced in PATTERN BOOKS from the early seventeenth century onwards. They were following a well-established tradition: Sebastiano Serlio (1474–1554) began to publish his seven books of architecture in 1537. This fully illustrated record of the buildings of the ancients with details, plans and elevations was immediately taken up, first in the Netherlands and thence to England, inspiring the use of Classical Renaissance ornament in buildings across northern Europe. Later works, significantly VITRUVIUS BRITTANICUS, published by Colen Campbell in 1715, disseminated the increasingly resolved rules of Palladianism and illustrated ARCHITECTURAL MODELS from which architects might, and did, derive their own designs.

Other homages are more piecemeal. SIR EDWIN LUTYENS (1869–1944) adopted many of the architectural tricks of Sir John Vanbrugh (1664–1726). The Baroque master's heavy rustication, articulated massing, muscular pilasters and applied columns are used 250 years later in Edwardian country houses as responses to architectural ancestry rather than wholesale revivals. The Gothic Revival of the mid-nineteenth century was one that, in harmony with that period's greedy appetite for decoration and stylistic eclecticism, tended to collect specific quotations from different precedents: a tower here, a spire there, some tracery from somewhere else. Its great architects – Pugin, Butterfield, Burges and Street – created a synergy of the Gothic that was at once backward-looking and something quite new. Sometimes architectural models are reduced into miniature but on other occasions they are expanded. Recently the Duchess of Cornwall pub in Poundbury, Dorset – the whole village itself a copybook of derivation and example – is an amplified response by Quinlan and Francis Terry Architects to Henry Bell's Custom House of 1683 in King's Lynn, Norfolk.

The phenomenon of recording architectural models relied on observation and analytical measured drawings, stone by stone, volute by acanthus scroll, frieze by architrave. The copybooks were freely published and purchased both by the leading architects of the day and by less erudite readers, speculative builders and developers. In the hands of lesser and often unnamed designers the language and grammar of the ancient models is often garbled, even misunderstood, but frequently to great effect. All over England, town halls and theatres, baths and assembly rooms quote freely and inaccurately. This treatment, ARTISAN MANNERISM, can add lively and energetic interpretations of the models even when heading some way away from the original.

Whether a Ptolemaic Egyptian temple reworked as a factory in west London, a villa in the Veneto translated into the White House in Washington or a Pagan temple devoted to Athena reinterpreted as a church dedicated to St Mary Magdalen, Western architecture from the late fifteenth century until the mid-twentieth century involved the rethinking and development of earlier styles. Certain buildings represented these periods profoundly and so these ARCHETYPES become especially significant to students of architecture, as well as interesting to identify whether in direct reproduction or more tangential allusion.

The PARTHENON. The ULTIMATE ARCHETYPE, built
by PERICLES 447-432 BC. RELIEFS in Pediment & Frieze
carved by PHIDIAS. Architects allegedly IKTINOS &
CALLICRATES. It is the basis for many buildings
around The World

The ERECHTHEUM. 421~406 BC. The porch supported by CARYATIDS
(The Girls). One of The originals (These ones in Athens are copies)
can be seen in The BRITISH MUSEUM, one of The Elgin Marbles
'saved' by The WISE/INFAMOUS Lord Elgin in 1801-12

As well as being The perfect DORIC TEMPLE, it is a good example of SITE-SPECIFIC building dominating The already COMMANDING Acropolis in ATHENS

The ATHENIAN TREASURY, DELPHI · 490BC · Built To commemorate The BATTLE of MARATHON

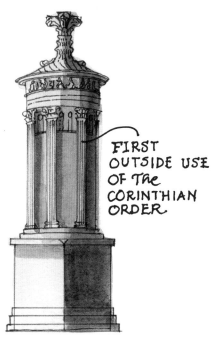

FIRST OUTSIDE USE OF THE CORINTHIAN ORDER

The CHORAGIC MONUMENT of LYSICRATES, below the Acropolis ATHENS 335-334 BC

was the model for

PORTA BORSARI · VERONA 1st CENTURY AD

The Maison CARRÉE · NÎMES, France, The Best preserved of all ANCIENT TEMPLES The model for The MADELEINE (Paris) GO ON LOOK IN THE TEXT

The DUGALD STEWART Monument · EDINBURGH 1831 (AD...)

PONT du GARD ~ France · 40-60 AD. N.B. These CLASSICAL BUILDINGS represent an INTERNATIONAL Style used THROUGHOUT The ROMAN Empire for Centuries

Temple of Horus · 237-57 BC · EDFU, Egypt. These Buildings from well outside The classical tradition inspired revivals from Paris To Penzance (The Egyptian House 1835-6)

The MODEL is used again (see Page 181) for the HOOVER Building. Wallis, Gilbert & Partners, 1933. Perivale · London

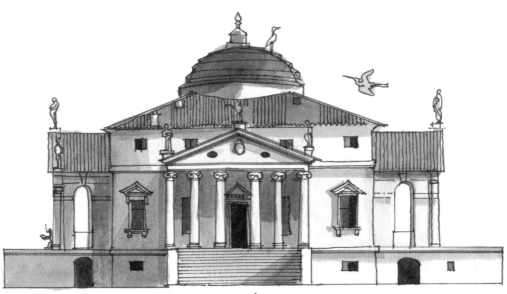

VILLA CAPRA, called 'la Rotonda'. Andrea PALLADIO 1567. After Palladio's death in 1580 The building was completed by Vincenzo Scamozzi. The shallow dome was inspired by The Pantheon. This remains a MUCH copied building

The TEMPIETO built on the site ascribed to the crucifixion of St Peter. Designed by BRAMANTE 1481-1500. This is a most INFLUENTIAL building on The North European Baroque (Think St Pauls...)

The OBELISK of HATSHEPSUT. KARNAK, Luxor, Egypt 1513-1458 BC (23m Tall, it's a big one...) The Vogue for things Egyptian was stimulated by Napoleon's Campaign in Egypt (1798-1801) & The Obelisk became an important component in neo-classical compositions

The SPHINX of HATSHEPSUT now safe in The Metropolitan in New York. another part of The Egyptian Schtick...

The PANTHEON in Rome. 126 AD. Built on the site of an earlier temple. The MASSIVE DOME makes this one of the most Dramatic INTERIORS in the world. The OCELLUS in the Roof letting in LIGHT & a tiny bit of rain

CONSTANTINE'S ARCH. Rome, Dedicated 315 AD. using some earlier material. (The model for Hyde Park's Marble Arch.)

EXEMPLARS

SOME BUILDINGS TO VISIT

DUNFERMLINE ABBEY
FIFE

ST PETER'S · BRADWELL
ESSEX

THE JEWS HOUSE · LINCOLN · LINCS

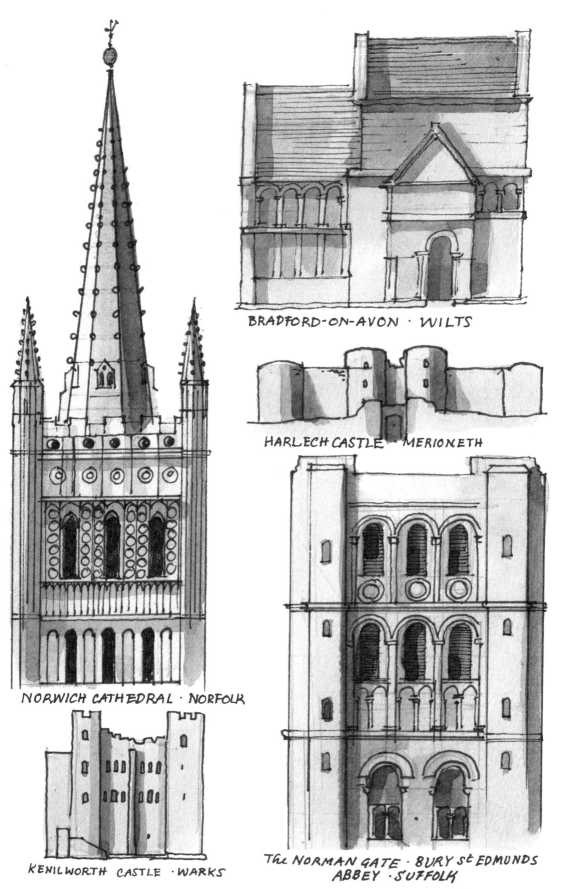

BRADFORD-ON-AVON · WILTS

HARLECH CASTLE · MERIONETH

NORWICH CATHEDRAL · NORFOLK

KENILWORTH CASTLE · WARKS

The NORMAN GATE · BURY St EDMUNDS
ABBEY · SUFFOLK

TRETOWER COURT · BRECKS

BAYLEAF. SINGLETON · W·SUSSEX

HADDON HALL · DERBY.

GREAT CHALFIELD MANOR · WILTS

. MARY'S · BEVERLEY · YORKS

OXBURGH HALL · NORFOLK

BOSTON STUMP · LINCS

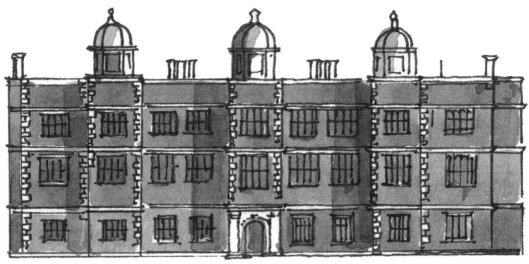

DODDINGTON HALL · LINCS

BURLEIGH HOUSE · LINCS

LORD LEYCESTER HOSPITAL · WARKS

HENGRAVE HALL · SUFFOLK

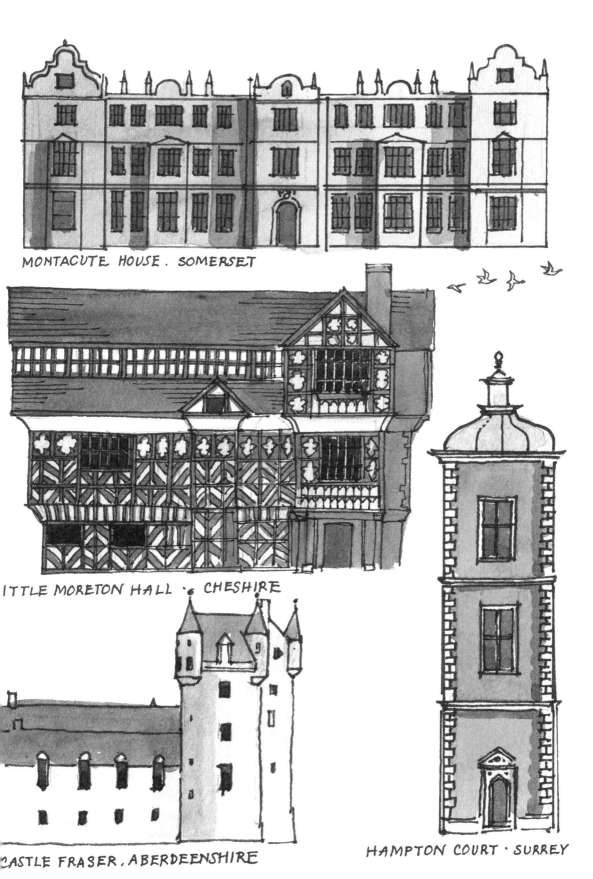

MONTACUTE HOUSE · SOMERSET

ITTLE MORETON HALL · CHESHIRE

CASTLE FRASER, ABERDEENSHIRE

HAMPTON COURT · SURREY

(at) CHISWICK HOUSE · LONDON

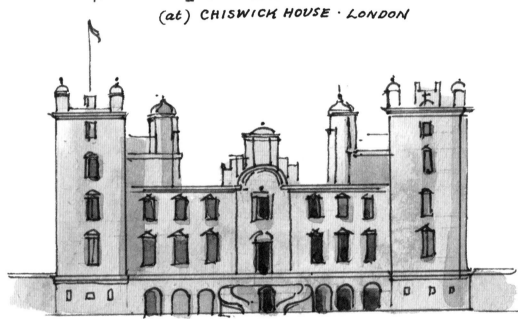

DRUMLANRIG CASTLE · DUMFRIES

ASTON HALL · WARKS

WILTON HOUSE · WILTS

The BANQUETING HOUSE · LONDON

GLAMIS CASTLE · ANGUS

SEATON DELAVAL HALL · NORTHUMBS

TREDEGAR HOUSE · MONMOUTHSHIRE

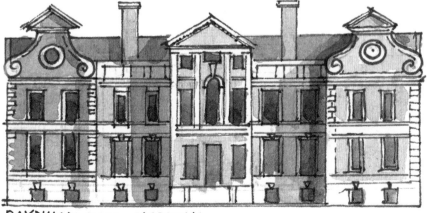

RAYNHAM HALL · NORFOLK

ST BENET · PAUL
WHARF · LONDON

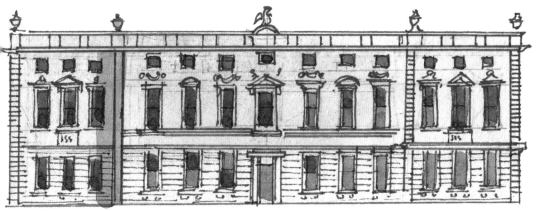

DYRHAM PARK · GLOS

HOUSE of DUN · ANGUS

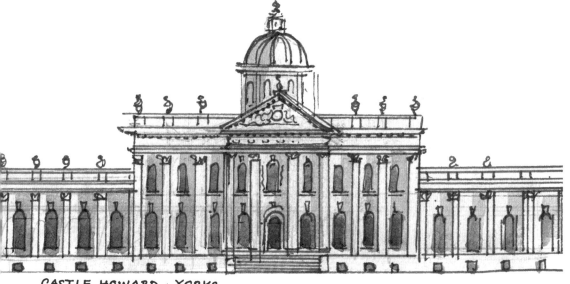

CASTLE HOWARD · YORKS

HOLKHAM HALL · NORFOLK

WEST WYCOMBE PARK · BUCKS

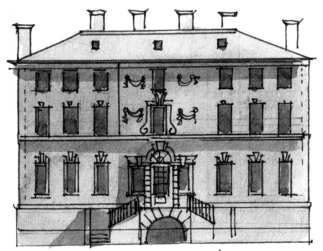

POLLOK HOUSE · GLASGOW

CHISWICK HOUSE · MIDDX

SHUGBOROUGH HALL · STAFFS

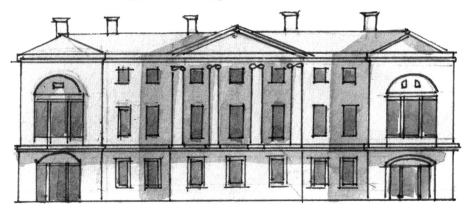

SLEDMERE HOUSE · YORKS

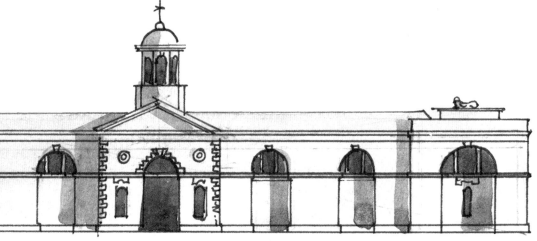

STABLES · NEWBY HALL · YORKS

TRENTHAM MAUSOLEUM · STAFFS

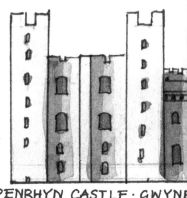

PENRHYN CASTLE · GWYNE

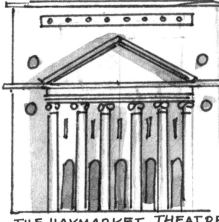

THE HAYMARKET THEATRE
LONDON

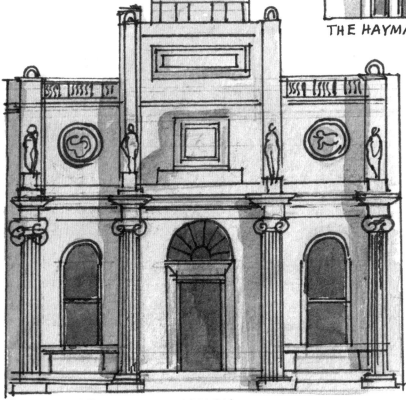

PITSHANGER MANOR · MIDDX

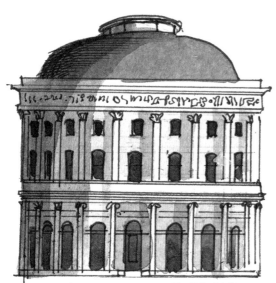

ICKWORTH HOUSE · SUFFOLK

The NATIONAL GALLERY
EDINBURGH

The GRECIAN HOUSE · COCKERMOUTH · CUMBS

ST MARY & ST NICHOLAS · WILTON · WILTS

DUNROBIN CASTLE · SUTHERLAND

BYLAUGH HALL · NORFOLK

HIGHCLERE CASTLE · BERKS

OSBORNE HOUSE I. OF. W

ST GEORGE'S St · GLASGOW

SCARISBRICK HALL · LANCS

TYNTESFIELD · SOMERSET

The NICHOLSON Institute
LEEK ·STAFFS

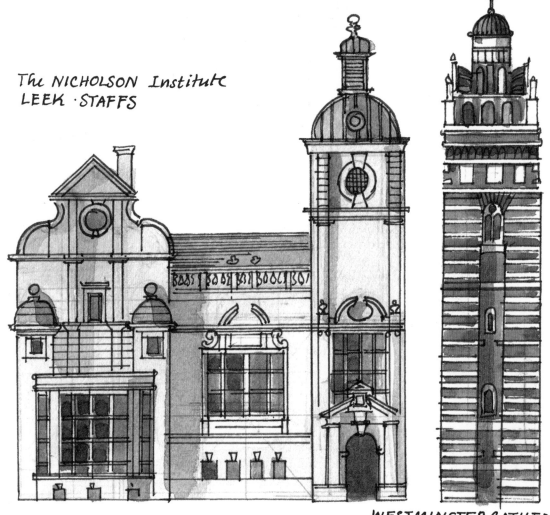

WESTMINSTER CATHEDR

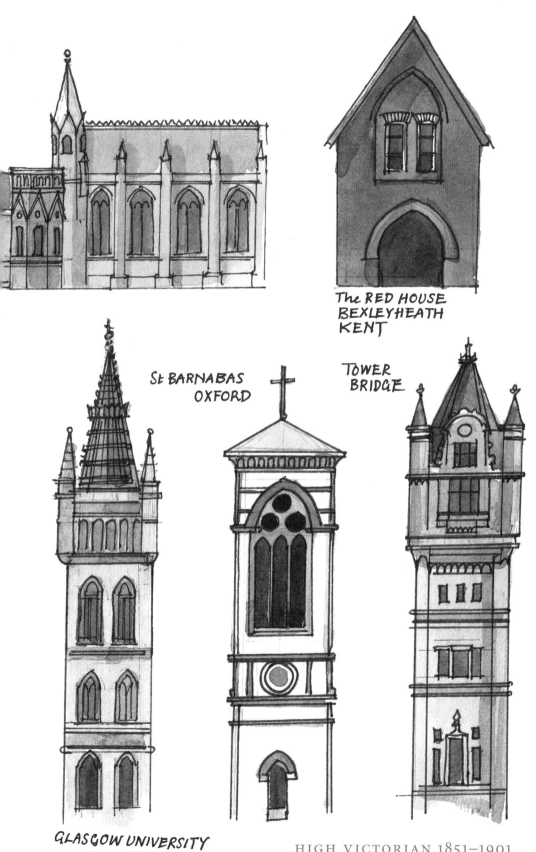

The RED HOUSE
BEXLEYHEATH
KENT

St BARNABAS
OXFORD

TOWER
BRIDGE

GLASGOW UNIVERSITY

MEMORIAL LIBRARY · BEDALES SCHOOL · HANTS

CASTLE DROGO · DEVON

BROADLEYS · CUMBS

HILL HOUSE · GLASGOW

The GEM CINEMA · YARMOUTH · NORFOLK

LINDISFARNE CASTLE
NORTHUMBS

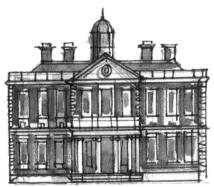

STANSTED PARK · W·SUSSEX

THe SUN HOUSE · LONDON

U.E.A. BUILDING · NORFOLK

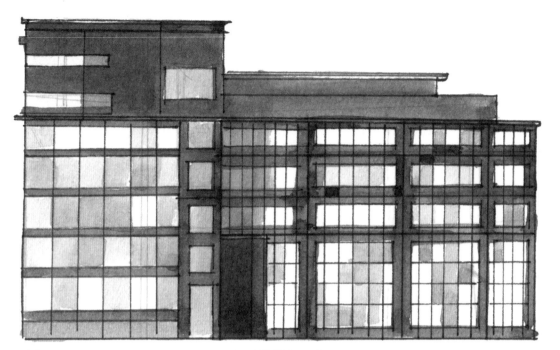

THE EXPRESS BUILDING · MANCHESTER

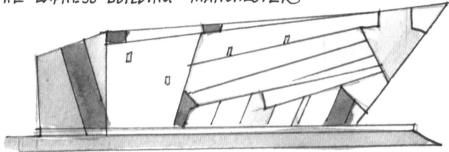

THE DEEP · HULL · YORKS

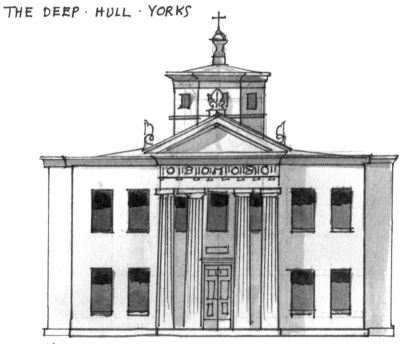

VILLA · REGENT'S PARK
LONDON

STONE

It is possible to quarry stone from areas throughout Britain, but it's only worth quarrying if the stone weathers to an acceptable colour and can be cut, dressed or carved satisfactorily. Among the types that pass these tests are BATH STONE, which comes from the great oolite limestone quarries in Wiltshire, Somerset and Gloucestershire, and COTSWOLD STONE, which takes its name from the hills in which it is found. Both have a distinctive honey colour. YORK STONE, obtained from carboniferous sandstone quarries in Yorkshire, can be cut very thin, so is most often used for paving.

In the past, local stone was generally chosen for building purposes because it did not have to be transported long distances. HEADINGTON STONE, local to Oxford, was used for many early buildings in that city, and Edinburgh New Town (not that new now, as it's actually Georgian) used a dun-coloured stone from nearby Craigleith. However, high-status buildings sometimes used materials from quite distant places. Stonehenge, for example, used WELSH BLUESTONE; Windsor Castle and Eton College used RAGSTONE from Hythe in Kent; Carlisle Cathedral was built of RED SANDSTONE from the Bunter quarry in the Midlands; and Canterbury Cathedral used stone imported from Normandy.

Later on, fashion also influenced the choice of material. Sir Christopher Wren used PURBECK and PORTLAND STONE from Dorset for his churches, while others developed a taste for SCOTTISH GRANITE. Very often the buildings would be roofed with WELSH SLATE, an enduringly popular material.

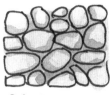

RANDOM RUBBLE

COURSED RUBBLE

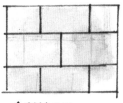

ASHLAR

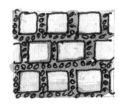

GALLETING

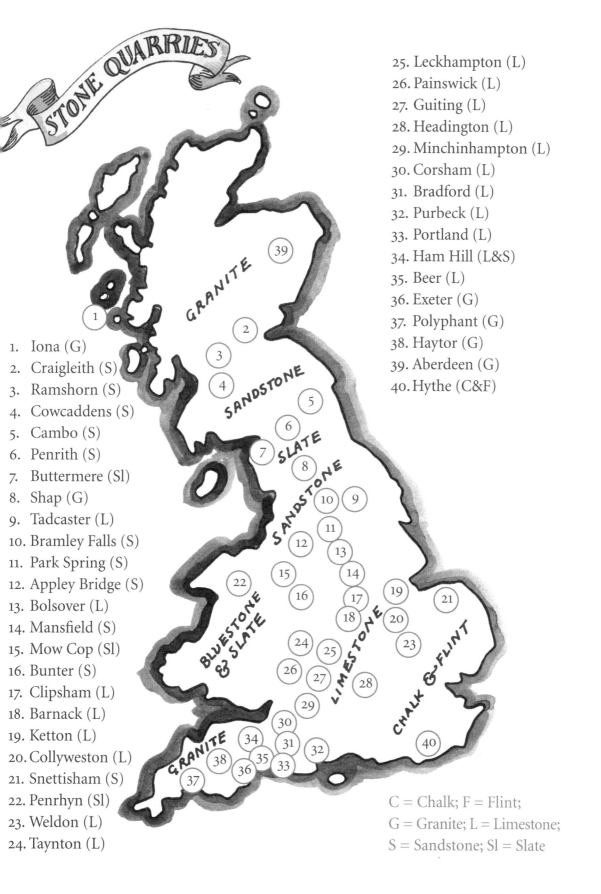

STONE QUARRIES

1. Iona (G)
2. Craigleith (S)
3. Ramshorn (S)
4. Cowcaddens (S)
5. Cambo (S)
6. Penrith (S)
7. Buttermere (Sl)
8. Shap (G)
9. Tadcaster (L)
10. Bramley Falls (S)
11. Park Spring (S)
12. Appley Bridge (S)
13. Bolsover (L)
14. Mansfield (S)
15. Mow Cop (Sl)
16. Bunter (S)
17. Clipsham (L)
18. Barnack (L)
19. Ketton (L)
20. Collyweston (L)
21. Snettisham (S)
22. Penrhyn (Sl)
23. Weldon (L)
24. Taynton (L)
25. Leckhampton (L)
26. Painswick (L)
27. Guiting (L)
28. Headington (L)
29. Minchinhampton (L)
30. Corsham (L)
31. Bradford (L)
32. Purbeck (L)
33. Portland (L)
34. Ham Hill (L&S)
35. Beer (L)
36. Exeter (G)
37. Polyphant (G)
38. Haytor (G)
39. Aberdeen (G)
40. Hythe (C&F)

C = Chalk; F = Flint;
G = Granite; L = Limestone;
S = Sandstone; Sl = Slate

The brickmaking skills of the ROMANS were lost as the last legions scuttled home in the fifth century AD. Examples remain in Roman walls such as those at Burgh Castle, Norfolk. These bricks are huge, 18in long, 12in wide and about 1½in thick. It was not until the late MEDIEVAL period that brick building returned in a significant way.

In the pre-industrial age, brickmaking was LOCAL, which led to great regional variation. The bricks of Holkham Hall in Norfolk, for example, are made of a yellow gault clay completely different from the soft orange material of the outbuildings at nearby Houghton Hall. Similarly, the rather ugly, hard, bluey-red clays of the Midlands are characteristic of buildings in that area, and when such bricks came to be seen elsewhere, after the railways made bulk transport of materials a reality in the nineteenth century, they seemed strangely ill at ease.

The SIZE of bricks also varied. Tudor bricks were smaller than those of the eighteenth century, and it was only when brick taxes were imposed that a regularity of size became normal. The dimensions changed based on whether bricks were taxed by number (post-1784 Brick Tax), which would incline them to grow in size, or by volume (post-1803), which would incline them to be smaller as you would get more bricks for your ton of clay.

Decorative brickwork, a style developed to a high degree in the Netherlands, is typical of the seventeenth century, and again rose to prominence with the Queen Anne Revival in the nineteenth century.

DIAPERING with burnt headers

HERRINGBONE

ENGLISH BOND

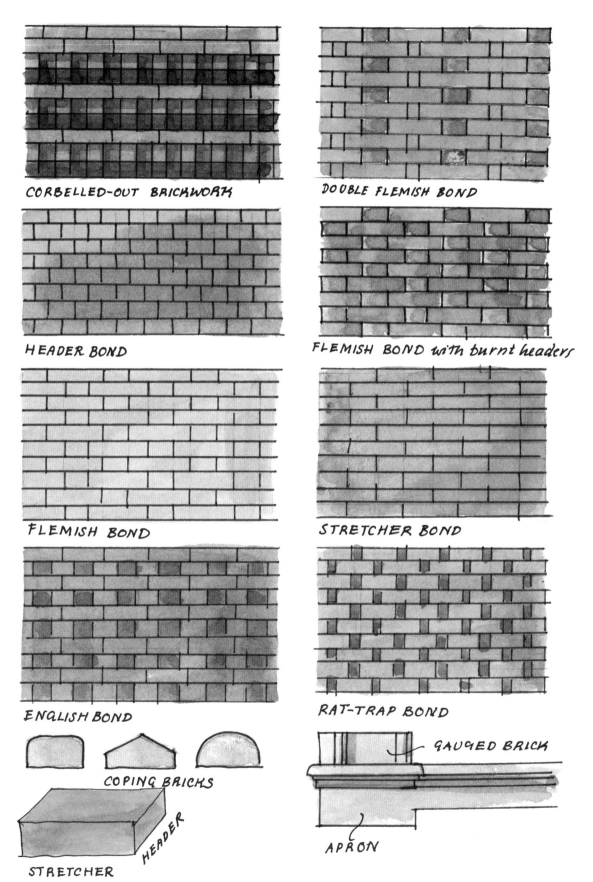

CORBELLED-OUT BRICKWORK

DOUBLE FLEMISH BOND

HEADER BOND

FLEMISH BOND with burnt headers

FLEMISH BOND

STRETCHER BOND

ENGLISH BOND

RAT-TRAP BOND

COPING BRICKS

GAUGED BRICK

STRETCHER

HEADER

APRON

TILES

The use of CLAY tiles and TERRACOTTA ornament is widespread. Clay is easier to work than stone and, when fired correctly, can be just as long lasting. In the Tudor and Jacobean periods, terracotta was used for both isolated decoration and as a more general wall covering among brickwork. The material fell from grace until the Queen Anne Revival, when public buildings such as pubs used terracotta lettering.

Mathematical tiles are tiles that imitate bricks. Their light weight and thin profile made them suitable for refacing timber-framed buildings. Tile cladding crossed into polite architecture from vernacular building with the Arts and Crafts movement.

Tiles are, of course, most frequently used on the roof. There are two sorts: flat PEG tiles and PANTILES. These pans quickly replaced basic peg tiles in eastern Britain. On high-status buildings, they were usually glazed black.

Thinner ones, known as Roman tiles, are often used in warehouses and factories.

ASSORTED TERRACOTTA PANELS

PAN TILE

ROMAN TILE

SCALLOPED & STRAIGHT
TILE HANGING

PEG TILE

ROUND-HEADED
PEG TILE

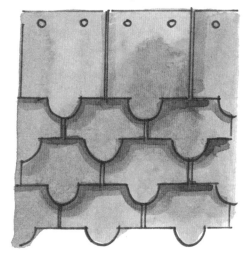

SCALLOPED TILE HANGING

MATHEMATICAL STRETCHER

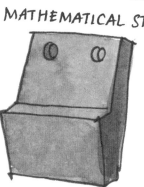

MATHEMATICAL HEADER

MATHEMATICAL
TILES

TIMBER

Most of Britain is well timbered, and in all but the most inhospitable spots wood plays an important role in buildings. However, except for large timber-framed manor houses in the Midlands and the Welsh Marches, such as Little Moreton Hall, timber rarely made the transition to sole building material.

It is in the construction of the ROOF that timber is most important. In later buildings, this means it is all but invisible, but in earlier work that is far from the case. Churches and cathedrals, halls that are open to the roof, and barns, such as the thirteenth-century Great Coxwell, Oxfordshire, all show their powerful timber trusses or elaborately carved hammerbeams.

The style was revived in the Arts and Crafts movement, and is best shown in Ernest Gimson's memorial library at Bedales School, Hampshire, where pairs of massive crucks form a nave and aisles.

COLLAR

KING POST

RAFTER

TIE BEAM

BR

JETTY

PLAT

BRESSUMER

STUD

QUATREFOIL PANEL

PANELS

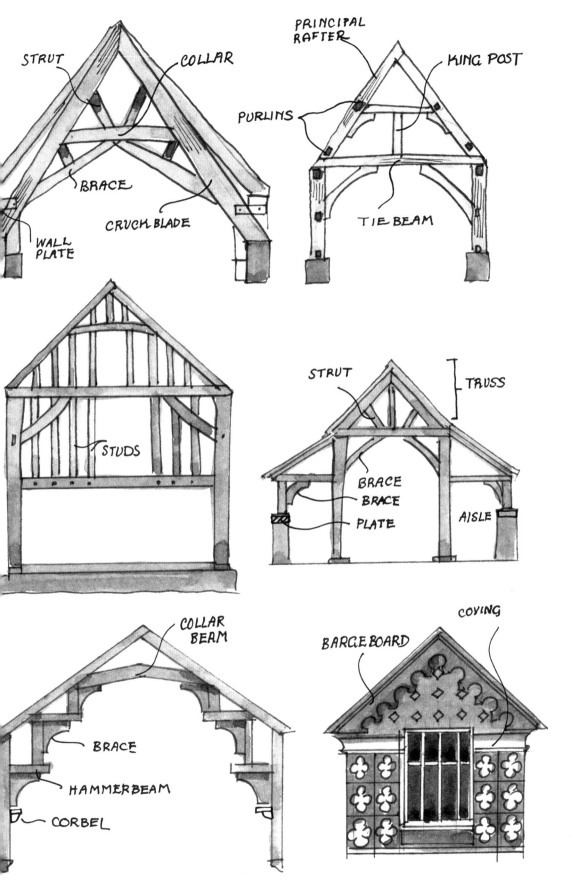

STRUT

COLLAR

PRINCIPAL RAFTER

KING POST

PURLINS

BRACE

CRUCK BLADE

WALL PLATE

TIE BEAM

STUDS

STRUT

TRUSS

BRACE

BRACE PLATE

AISLE

COLLAR BEAM

COVING

BARGEBOARD

BRACE

HAMMERBEAM

CORBEL

Robert Smythson (1535–1614)
Inigo Jones (1573–1652)
John Webb (1611–72)
Sir Roger Pratt (1620–85)
Hugh May (1621–84)
Sir Christopher Wren (1632–1723)
William Talman (1650–1719)
Nicholas Hawksmoor (1661–1736)
Sir John Vanbrugh (1664–1726)
Thomas Archer (1668–1743)
William Kent (1685–1748)
Lord Burlington (1694–1753)
Colen Campbell (1676–1729)
James Gibbs (1682–1754)
William Adam (1689–1748)
John Wood (1704–54)
James 'Athenian' Stuart (1713–88)
Horace Walpole (1717–97)
William Chambers (1722–96)
John Wood (the younger) (1728–81)
Robert Adam (1728–92)
Jeffry Wyatt (1746–1813)
John Nash (1752–1835)
S. P. Cockerell (1753–1827)
Sir John Soane (1753–1837)
William Wilkins (1778–1839)
Philip Hardwick (1792–1870)
Sir Charles Barry (1795–1860)
Decimus Burton (1800–81)
Isambard Kingdom Brunel
  (1806–59)

George Gilbert Scott (1811–78)
Augustus W. N. Pugin (1812–52)
William Butterfield (1814–1900)
Alfred Waterhouse (1815–98)
Benjamin Woodward (1816–61)
John Ruskin (1819–1900)
G. E. Street (1824–81)
Norman Shaw (1831–1912)
J. J. Stevenson (1831–1908)
Philip Webb (1831–1915)
William Morris (1834–96)
Basil Champneys (1842–1935)
Aston Webb (1849–1930)
E. S. Prior (1852–1932)
Frank Matcham (1854–1920)
George Skipper (1856–1948)
William Lethaby (1857–1931)
Charles Voysey (1857–1941)
Ernest Gimson (1864–1919)
Charles Rennie Mackintosh
  (1868–1928)
Sir Edwin Lutyens (1869–1944)
Walter Gropius (1883–1969)
Ludwig Mies van der Rohe
  (1886–1969)
Le Corbusier (1887–1965)
Erich Mendelsohn (1887–1953)
Hans 'Hannes' Meyer
  (1889–1954)
Serge Chermayeff (1900–96)
Berthold Lubetkin (1901–90)
Albert Speer (1905–81)
Sir Denys Lasdun (1914–2001)
Lord Richard Rogers (B. 1933)
Sir Norman Foster (B. 1935)
John Quinlan Terry (B. 1937)
Renzo Piano (B. 1937)
Sir Terry Farrell (B. 1938)

REIGNS OF KINGS & QUEENS

MEDIEVAL
William I (1066–1087)
William II (1087–1100)
Henry I (1100–1135)
Stephen (1135–1154)
Henry II (1154–1189)
Richard I (1189–1199)
John (1199–1216)
Henry III (1216–1272)
Edward I (1272–1307)

LATE MEDIEVAL
Edward II (1307–1327)
Edward III (1327–1377)
Richard II (1377–1399)
Henry IV (1399–1413)
Henry V (1413–1422)
Henry VI (1422–1461)
Edward IV (1461–1483)
Richard III (1483–1485)

TUDOR & ELIZABETHAN
Henry VII (1485–1509)
Henry VIII (1509–1547)
Edward VI (1547–1553)
Mary I (1553–1558)
Elizabeth I (1558–1603)

JACOBEAN
James I (1603–1625)

CAROLINE & QUEEN ANNE
Charles I (1625–1649)
Commonwealth (1649–1660)
Charles II (1660–1685)
James II (1685–1688)
William and Mary (1689– 1702)
Anne (1702–1714)

GEORGIAN
George I (1714–1727)
George II (1727–1760)
George III (1760–1820)

REGENCY
George IV (1820–1830)
William IV (1830–1837)

VICTORIAN
Victoria (1837–1901)

EDWARDIAN
Edward VII (1901–1910)

MODERN
George V (1910–1936)
Edward VIII (1936, abdicated)
George VI (1936–1952)
Elizabeth II (1952–present)

INDEX OF PEOPLE

INDEX of PLACES

INDEX of TERMS

THANKS

This is obviously a book of complete pleasure and fun. An excuse to spend ages drawing hundreds of buildings and writing about them is hard to find, for which I have to thank my agent Caroline Dawnay and my editor at Bloomsbury, Richard Atkinson. Thank you to the kind and lovely Natalie Bellos who has beaten a path through the thorny mess of text and scribbled captions that I handed in. Also thanks to Octavia Pollock who has obliterated some of the grosser inaccuracies from the book and pointed out gaping omissions.

I am, as ever, grateful beyond description to my friend and teacher Alastair Langlands, general polymath, who has discussed, researched and corrected everything in this book; and also to an anonymous helper with whom I first produced a proto-primer in 1978. So grievous are my ignorant omissions that his or her name must remain a mystery.

The book would never have come into being if kind Jeremy Musson had not commissioned the Architectural Cribs series for *Country Life* – his idea completely, and the inspiration for this book – and indeed if Mark Hedges, the magazine's editor, had not been as enthusiastic and supportive.

William Whittaker, my saintly assistant at Emma Bridgewater Ltd, has tidied, neatened and generally scrubbed up my messy work for which I am utterly grateful. Peter Dawson, the designer, has drawn together the various elements with great skill.

But without the sharp eye and excoriatingly critical approach of my wife Emma Bridgewater, who put up with the wilful distraction from our other work, this book would definitely not exist.